AF669677

DISCOVER YOUR VOICE

Rama Vaidyanathan is an audiologist and speech language and voice pathologist. After completing her graduation in audiology and speech therapy in 1985, and master's in linguistics in 1989 from Mumbai University, she has been working as a specialist in voice training for over twenty-five years. She has been a voice trainer for several well-known TV and film personalities such as Sonakshi Sinha, Neeti Mohan, Nina Manuel, Pia Trivedi, Sheetal Malhar, Sudesh Bhosale, Allu Arjun, Perizaad Zorabian, Shriya Saran and several others. She has also worked in Whistling Woods International Institute as a voice trainer. She prides her association with the Shankar Mahadevan Academy, for whom she has designed and teaches a course called Voice Gym. Rama is an expert in not only voice care, but also in effective use of voice, voice projection, voice endurance, voice modulation, diction, accent correction and dialogue delivery.

Praise for Rama Vaidyanathan

'I know Rama ma'am for more than fifteen years. She introduced me to voice culture, breathing techniques and taught how to maintain good vocal health. Her guidance has helped me grow as a singer. She is one of the finest voice coaches in Mumbai. I wish success for her book and hope she keeps inspiring people just the way she inspires me!' – *Neeti Mohan, singer*

'*Discover Your Voice* is an excellent companion for those looking to finetune their voice .The perfect guide for actors, singers and others who use their voice for their profession! I have learnt a lot about my voice from the book and from Rama.' – *Shriya Saran, actress*

'Voice training is a must for every actor to take their performance to the next level. I have changed my dialogue delivery, dubbing style and the way I use my voice after taking training from Rama.' – *Allu Arjun, actor*

'For any actor, voice is a very unique part of their personality and identity. For an actor to become a star, a lot of things are needed, and a good voice and excellent dialogue delivery are definitely two of those things. Actors work very hard, and spend a lot of time and effort in training themselves ... One area which they should never neglect is their voice and speech. Two factors help an actor instantly connect with the audience and form a bond: their eyes and voice. I would seriously advise all upcoming actors to invest some time and energy in training their voice, and to develop a strong, flexible voice, and to work hard on their dialogue delivery skills, as this will go a long way in ensuring [their] success. I know that speaking or talking comes naturally to us, but what many new actors don't realize is that delivering dialogues is not the same as speaking. It's a totally different ball game, and one needs to be trained and developed.' – *Arbaaz Khan, actor, producer and director*

'In this superficial world, everyone is on the lookout for pretty things ... a pretty face, a good figure, great clothes and a great voice. As an actor it is essential to have a good voice. If you have a voice that is alluring to people, you are one step closer to getting that coveted role. People don't want to hear someone talk if their voice is too loud, not articulate, or if they speak too fast or too slow, or with a lisp.' – *Ashmit Patel, actor*

'An actor's voice is a part of their persona. Can you imagine Dilip Kumar without his soft, rhythmic speech or Amitabh Bachchan without the baritone? It is an unmistakeable instrument of their trade! It needs cultivation and care. An actor may have the body of a god, but at least they must have the voice of an angel!' – *Roshan Abbas, anchor, director*

DISCOVER YOUR VOICE

A Step-by-Step Guide to Unleashing The Power of Your Voice

RAMA VAIDYANATHAN

HarperCollins *Publishers* India

First published in India in 2016 by
HarperCollins *Publishers* India
HarperCollins Publishers India, Cyber City, Building 10-A, Gurugram,
Haryana-122002, India
www.harpercollins.co.in

2 4 6 8 10 9 7 5 3 1
Copyright © Rama Vaidyanathan 2016

P-ISBN: 978-93-5264-136-9
E-ISBN: 978-93-5264-137-6

Rama Vaidyanathan asserts the moral right
to be identified as the author of this work.

The views and opinions expressed in this book
are the author's own and the facts are as reported by her,
and the publishers are not in any way liable for the same.

All rights reserved. No part of this publication may be reproduced,
stored in a retrieval system, or transmitted, in any form or by any means,
electronic, mechanical, photocopying, recording or otherwise,
without the prior permission of the publishers.

Without limiting the exclusive rights of any author, contributor or the publisher of this publication, any unauthorized use of this publication to train generative artificial intelligence (AI) technologies is expressly prohibited. HarperCollins also exercise their rights under Article 4(3) of the Digital Single Market Directive 2019/790 and expressly reserve this publication from the text and data-mining exception.

Typeset in 11.5/14.5 Requiem by
R. Ajith Kumar

Printed and bound at
MicroPrints India, New Delhi

MIX
Paper
FSC FSC® C218906

This product is made of FSC®-certified and other controlled material.

HarperCollins Publishers, Macken House, 39/40 Mayor Street
Upper, Dublin 1, D01 C9W8, Ireland

This book is dedicated to Partap Sharma, Dinesh Thakur and Nandu Bhende, three people who were my mentors, colleagues and associates in my journey. I miss having them around but I know their blessings are always with me.

CONTENTS

FOREWORD

A teacher for singers, actors and teachers – that's how one can best describe Rama Vaidyanathan's profession. It's the advantage of being a specialist in a field where not many people have ventured in the past.

At the Shankar Mahadevan Academy, we are very privileged to have Rama as part of our faculty. *Discover Your Voice* is a book that's one level deeper than learning music or any art form. It talks about how to maintain and develop the voice, the primary instrument which lets you sing and speak, and utilize it to its full potential. It so happens that most of us, even if we are singers, actors, public speakers, do not use our voice and vocal cords optimally. It's a bit like a sportsman playing a sport without doing proper warm-up exercises such as bending, stretching, etc. Voice training is actually like golf – it is not about how hard you hit the ball, it is about using the right technique to get the required distance, flight, etc.

This book can open up a new thought process for all those who utilize their voice on a daily basis and get them thinking about newer methods of using their vocal cords and develop the correct technique in order to get amazing results. I particularly like the fact that Rama has devoted an entire chapter on breathing, perhaps the most underrated activity that lets us sing well. Breathing and singing are completely interconnected and one depends on the other. If you get your breathing technique right then you can sing with ease!

As a singer and music composer, I congratulate and thank Rama for her path-breaking effort in making people understand the principles of voice technique, something most of us are ignorant about and do not give due importance.

Lots of love and good wishes.

SHANKAR MAHADEVAN

INTRODUCTION

As a child, like every south Indian girl, I started learning Indian classical music, and thus began my love affair with *voice*. As I sang, I soon realized that it was very important to train your voice if you wanted to sing well. Although I kept asking my teachers and gurus for tips on how to develop a great voice, sadly, I never quite found the precise guidance and knowledge which I sought. Singing, just like acting, puts a tremendous amount of stress upon your voice; my voice often gave up on me and I found that I was unable to use all my music training and knowledge to sing as well as I wanted to, or as well as I was capable of. I also noticed that many of the students who were learning music, including myself, would frequently develop a hoarse voice due to the inappropriate use of the vocal cords. Later, during my interactions with many actors as their voice coach, these sentiments were echoed by them as well, and they had no clue about how to prevent themselves from going hoarse!

From an early age I was also drawn to the movies and fell in love with cinema. I was always attracted to great voices and often wondered how some of those actors managed to have such powerful vocal cords and use them so effectively. It was a happy coincidence that I took up a course in speech and voice pathology as the subject for my graduation course. And once again, I entered the world of voice. I studied the scientific aspects of voice and began to deal with people who had problems with their voices. Now, as I began my education about voice and its scientific aspects, I started discovering many of the answers which I had been seeking since childhood.

I also came to understand that professional voice users like actors, singers, teachers, lawyers, voice-over professionals and others who use their voice a lot have the maximum amount of trouble with their voices. Apart from using their voices a lot due to the demands of their profession, they also tend to overuse or abuse their voices, sometimes pushing themselves to extreme limits. With this arose an ardent desire, almost a calling, to work with professional voice users, to help prevent their voice damage and train them in the proper usage of their larynges. As I started working with these people by training them in the proper use of their voice, thereby preventing voice problems, I also realized that there was this tremendous need to help them to effectively maximize the potential of their voices – in terms of voice modulation, voice endurance and voice projection. Since I also had a master's degree in linguistics and phonetics, I could easily help with any concerns about their diction and accent.

Thus began this beautiful journey of mine, training professional voice users and, in the process, learning a lot about the voice myself! It subsequently took me to Portland, USA, where I trained under the guidance of the renowned voice surgeon, Dr James P. Thomas. Although he mostly deals with voice pathology, his unique way of looking at, or rather hearing, the voice taught me a lot. I learnt to identify things about voice which would eventually make a huge difference in training one's voice. This journey also brought me to two wonderful associations and through them, lucrative work assignments – the two associations being the Shankar Mahadevan Music Academy for singers and Whistling Woods International Institute for actors.

The voice is, ironically, one of the most underrated aspects of a person's skill set. A professional voice user uses his voice day in and day out and tires it a lot. He uses his voice to express a gamut of emotions – happiness, sorrow, guilt, anger, etc. – and his voice becomes a key aspect of his identity and personality. As an actor, the voice is one of the vital tools of your trade, just like the face, hair, looks, body, expressivity, body language, dancing and fighting skills, etc. The same is true for a singer, teacher or lawyer. It is a crucial part of your armoury. And just as you hone all your other weapons or skills, you need to sharpen your voice skills as well in order to achieve super success and be complete in all aspects of your profession.

Having trained and worked with actors, singers and other professional voice users for the last twenty years and having perceived the dire need for scientific information and training in the area of voice, the idea of this book was born in my mind. I decided it was time I wrote something using all my knowledge and experience in this area so that more and more people can benefit from my expertise.

This book is written in a simple style and informal language. I imagined myself addressing my students while writing it, so it is more like a one-to-one interaction rather than a long monologue. I expect that anyone who reads this book thoroughly will be able to use his or her voice much more effectively.

In the following pages, I have explored all the scientific concepts and the various other aspects about voice that people would like to know. There is also has a complete step-by-step guide on the various exercises required to develop and maintain a good voice and to use it to its maximum potential. The book includes valuable quotes from important people in the world of voice that are a great source of inspiration and guidance for all voice users.

I hope you enjoy reading it and learn enough to enhance your skills.

PART ONE
GENERAL CONCEPTS
The Basic Ingredients

1

WHY SO MUCH NOISE ABOUT THE VOICE?

The Importance of Voice Training

We have all grown up listening to a host of great voices, be they actors, singers, sports commentators, radio announcers or comperes. These include Amitabh Bachchan, Dilip Kumar, Sanjeev Kumar, Om Puri, Naseeruddin Shah, Amrish Puri, Shabana Azmi, Rekha and many such fine actors. Or singers like Lata Mangeshkar, Mohammed Rafi, Kishore Kumar, Asha Bhosle, Manna Dey, or Mukesh. We also heard the enchanting voices of Ameen Sayani on radio, or Partap Sharma in the shows at Nehru Planetarium. All of us surely remember one or two teachers with excellent voices and speaking skills, which enabled us to remember concepts taught by them, even today.

Did you ever wonder how Mickey Mouse or Donald Duck spoke with such emotions? Did you wonder whose voices these were? What wonderful voice modulation they had? And you would laugh and cry and weep and even feel romantic as they spoke on the screen. The songs left you humming them all day long and touched your heart. You completely forgot that you were seeing Amitabh Bachchan or Rekha, instead you were watching their characters unfolding on the screen. And this was in an era where technical expertise was not as good as it is today. There was no sync sound, there were no pitch correctors, and yet, they sounded incredibly good. It was purely their voice control and finely honed skill of using their voices effectively. Also remember, most of them were never trained in the use of their voices.

It is not that there are no great voices of that calibre these days, of course there are! To find actors who are excellent in the use of their voices, we only need to look at Shah Rukh Khan, Aamir Khan, Hrithik Roshan, Salman Khan, Kareena Kapoor Khan, Akshay Kumar, Ajay Devgn, Aishwarya Rai Bachchan ... and many more. In the field of singing, there is Shankar Mahadevan, Sonu Nigam, Shreya Ghoshal, Arijit Singh and several others. These people are able to produce the same magic which the actors and singers and dubbing artists of the earlier generations did.

Although in today's world visual effects take precedence over audio, one cannot deny the fact that a good voice will always catch the attention of audiences. A lot of importance is being given to how good you look, in terms of well-sculpted bodies, designer clothes, great hairstyles, beautiful skin and make-up (in short, the visual aspect). There is nothing wrong in that. In fact, it only shows the excellence we have achieved in these fields. So much effort goes into achieving this perfection and it is brilliant. However, my only question is: why not put in the same effort in improving and perfecting your voice skills? I am not saying that the younger generation of today is not good with their voices; there are many who are fantastic. Nevertheless, there are several aspects of voice that are being carelessly overlooked today which could make the difference between a great performance or presentation and an average one. Many a time, the content of a chief executive officer's (CEO's) presentation may be brilliant, but if it is not presented well, it may run the risk of not being effective. The same is true for a newsreader. The news content across channels is similar; however, we still have our personal preferences of newsreaders, preferences which are governed mostly by their presentation skills.

One cannot deny the fact that unless the voices carry the emotions and convictions of what you are saying across to the audiences, you cannot connect to them. Therefore, if you need audiences in any field to be connected to you, you definitely need a strong and commanding voice.

Once when I was training a group of news presenters, someone asked me, 'If the content of my news is potent enough, why do I need presentation skills?' Research shows that 70 per cent of human attention, when someone speaks to you, is just on the quality of the voice, let alone your diction, modulation, accent, etc., and only then comes the content. Content is important, very important, and content actually guides voice modulation. Nevertheless, you cannot deny the fact that if you are in a room full of people and suddenly hear a very good voice, without a doubt you will look around to identify the source of that voice. A good voice creates a great impression. Good content by itself is sometimes not enough. How well you present it is also extremely important.

We know that a news presenter who speaks well increases viewership and is always given prime time on television. A good sports commentator can make even a dull game seem interesting. Brilliant animation is of limited use unless it is backed up by fantastic voicing skills. A lawyer who speaks well can sometimes win cases which seem difficult to win. A teacher with a good voice establishes a much better rapport with the student during his lecture. Therefore, although content is extremely important, it can be reinforced with far greater power with a great voice and effective speech skills.

What the audience hears is the content that you speak.

The various aspects of speech can be understood from Figure 1.1.

When I say voicing skills, it includes various aspects of voice and speech. Although these two are distinct entities, they cannot be separated. If speech is the building you are constructing then voice is its foundation, basement and lower floors.

This book has a detailed explanation of each of these above aspects, how to achieve a great voice, maintain it and use it maximally in your chosen profession.

Voice training is not an easily achievable task. There are many reasons for this. Firstly, it is a subtle skill, like

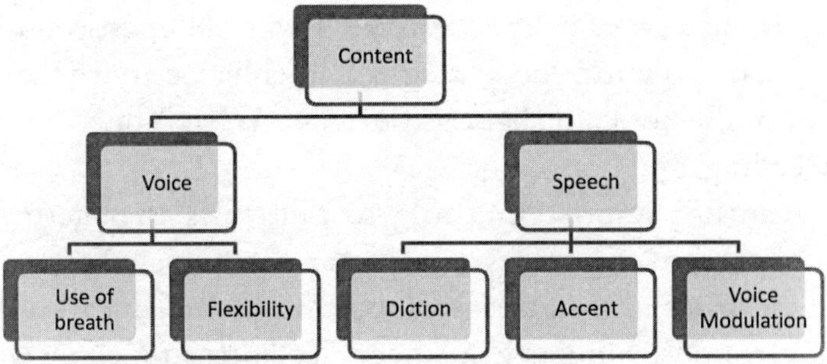

FIGURE 1.1: Various aspects of speech

music or singing. So, if you don't have a great aptitude for it, you have to put in a lot of effort, unlike someone who is naturally gifted. Secondly, your voice is your instrument here. And this instrument is a part of your body with various muscles, ligaments, cartilages, etc. Hence, unlike a violin or guitar, which can be tuned from the outside, this part needs physical training, like bodybuilding. Just as a good cricket or football player needs both physical fitness and game-specific skills, here too, you need to have good vocal fitness and application in various aspects of your speaking skills. Thirdly, unlike make-up, skin or hair, or your dressing skills, which someone else can do for you, this is something that you have to do yourself.

Your voice, apart from being an instrument or medium of communication, also reflects your personality, thinking, inner desires, anxieties, strengths and weaknesses. This is an aspect of voice which people are not commonly aware of. As a professional voice user, since your voice is such an important part of your repertoire, I will call upon you to work on this mind–body connect, to enhance your voice, later in the book, in chapter fourteen, 'What Your Voice Is Telling You'.

Another important thing to realize is that actors and voice-over professionals play various characters, personalities, ages, against various cultural and educational backgrounds. Similarly, a singer needs to sing songs at various pitches and for long stretches of time. A teacher has to speak to large, noisy groups for eight to ten hours a day. A lawyer requires to effectively build a case and put across points to convince the clients, the court and the judge. Newsreaders, sports commentators and comperes too verbalize and vocalize for sustained periods of time, sometimes having to use their voices to stir up their audiences to a fever pitch. A CEO or corporate executive uses his voice as a tool to convince his clients. Therefore, across a vast cross section of professions, there is a huge demand on your voice. You may need to analyse its various aspects from the tone to the accents, dialects, modulation, speed, pitch, volume, use of specific words or sounds, and so on.

Although speaking and using our voice comes naturally to us and we learn to speak as we grow up without really making any effort, you will by now have become aware that speaking as yourself, and using your voice professionally, to impact an audience, are two entirely different things. Don't make the mistake of assuming that it is just an extension of your natural speaking skills. So, if you train yourself in your voicing skills, it will make your job a lot easier and you can achieve your results effortlessly and in a very short span of time. But how do you know which areas are your weaknesses and which your strengths? I would urge you to do a self-analysis of your voice and decide which sections you need to work on. That is what the next chapter is all about.

2

LISTENING

A Quick Guide to What You Need to Work On

Your voice is your identity in sound. People recognize and know you by your voice. So you need to think about how your voice is at present, what you like about it and what you don't. Which areas do you want to improve upon?

Spend a day listening to your own voice. Pay special attention to your tone and words. Then write a brief description of your voice and the way you use it. You can also record it and then listen to it.

Having done that, you need to ask yourself the following questions. This is a very quick guide to assessing your voice; and with every question, I have pointed out the area you need to work on. This book has detailed chapters on all the areas pertaining to voice training.

DOES YOUR VOICE SOUND FLAT AND DULL, OR LIVELY AND ENERGETIC?

I am sure you've heard this being said a lot of times, 'Hey, you sound flat!' What does flat mean? Flat means sounding like a robot, like a machine, monotonous, dull and lifeless. It means that your voice lacks the normal cadences of intonation and also lacks expression and emotion. Voice modulation is the art of making your voice expressive. Some excellent examples of this would be Amjad Khan in *Sholay* or Amitabh Bachchan in the last scene of the film *Baghban*, or Partap Sharma's commentary at the Nehru Planetarium.

Let me elaborate. Voice modulation means having an expressive voice with all the emotions you want to portray. Normally, when we speak in our daily lives, we don't think about voice modulation because our emotions guide us through it. Hence, if you are angry you sound angry, if you are sad you sound sad, and so on. Since you are full of that emotion, it is automatically reflected in your voice.

But whilst at work, or dubbing a scene, you may or may not feel the emotions to the same degree as you would in your actual life, and hence your voice may not portray the sentiment to the required level. This is where techniques of voice modulation need to be brought into play so that passions and feelings are well manifested. Therefore, techniques like pause, stress, rhythm, pace, etc., need to be used. These are dealt with, in great detail, in the chapter on voice modulation with a step-by-step exercise guide.

DO YOU NEVER CHANGE THE TONE OF YOUR VOICE?

Then again, you need to work on modulation and also on the concepts of tonality and resonance. This is dealt with in detail in the chapter titled 'How to Get That Loud, Booming, Resonant Voice'. If you want to know what is good tonality and resonance, listen to Sanjeev Kumar in *Sholay* or listen to Arnab Goswami on Times Now.

DO YOU MUMBLE OR SPEAK TOO FAST?

Then you need to work on your diction. This is dealt with in detail in chapter seven, on diction. If you want to get an idea of excellent diction, listen to any of the dialogues of Shabana Azmi or Amitabh Bachchan, and observe the way they pronounce words.

ARE YOU TOO LOUD OR TOO SOFT?

Then you need to work on getting more control over your voice. It is like driving a car which is not responding well to the controls. This aspect has to do with the flexibility of your voice, which is dealt with in various chapters of this book.

DOES YOUR THROAT HURT WHEN YOU SHOUT OR SPEAK THE WHOLE DAY?

This means you have not learnt to use your breath,

that you are not speaking from your belly, and you are predominantly speaking from the throat. This is dealt with in detail in chapter three, titled 'Breathing'.

ARE YOU UNABLE TO PROJECT OR THROW YOUR VOICE?

This again is your inability to use your breath well and also about not having power in your voice. You can read all about this in chapter six, titled 'Voice Projection'. To get an idea of a really powerful voice, you should listen to Amrish Puri in any of his films.

DO YOU LEAVE OUT THE FINAL CONSONANTS IN WORDS?

This means you need to work on speech sharpness, diction and some vocal muscle strengthening exercises. You can get a good idea of sharp speech if you listen to actors like Raza Murad or Shabana Azmi.

DO YOU SOUND LIKE YOURSELF, AND NOT LIKE THE CHARACTER YOU ARE PORTRAYING?

What do you do if you are playing two characters, like father and son, or twin brothers? Or one character a villager and another an educated, sophisticated guy? Don't you have to sound different in each of these roles? Even in every role that you play, you need to sound different. If you look at

Tom Hanks, or rather listen to Tom Hanks, you will find that he sounds very different in each of his various roles. Or Amitabh Bachchan in *Aakhree Raasta* playing father and son. Or Govinda as uncle and nephew in *Haseena Maan Jaayegi*. Or Kamal Haasan in *Appu Raja*, *Chachi 420* and the Tamil film *Michael Madana Kamarajan*. These are a few examples to understand how great thespians sound like the characters that they play, and not like their real-life selves.

In order to do this, you need to have a repertoire of voice tones, qualities, accents, styles of voice and speech. This is dealt in detail in the section on voice styling, on page 141.

DOES THE NATIVE ACCENT OF YOUR MOTHER TONGUE INTRUDE INTO YOUR NORMAL SPEECH?

Accent is the flavour and feature of one language getting carried over to another language, unknowingly. Accent correction is a science dealing with phonetics. This is discussed in detail in the chapter eight, on accents.

DOES YOUR VOICE LACK THE MUCH DESIRED 'BARITONE'?

Baritone is nothing but a low-pitched voice and the pitch of the voice which is natural and God-given. It depends on physical aspects like the length and thickness of your vocal cords. So, if you don't have a baritone, it is quite a difficult task to acquire one. However, the good news is that it can be acquired through various exercises and is dealt with in detail in chapter five.

Apart from listening to your own voice, also listen to voices of people you meet and of those who you think have a great voice. I also want to tell you here that you should try and not just watch television, as the visual medium is far more overpowering than the auditory medium. You will miss out on the nuances of their speech and voice patterns. Keep your eyes closed, listen and try to catch the little nuances that people use in their voices.

In this chapter, I have dealt with all issues in brief, pertaining to your voice and speech. This helps you to go directly to that chapter which is of interest to you. However, I would urge you to read the chapter on breathing, which covers the basic concepts and also makes you understand the anatomy and physiology of voice, which are relevant to every aspect of having a great voice. And that is what the next chapter is all about.

3

BREATHING

Your Lifeline to Voice

Every activity that we undertake or perform in life depends on our ability to breathe. At birth, the first deep breath a baby takes comes out in the form of crying; indeed, all babies cry to come alive. This demonstrates how closely your voice and your breath are interconnected – you can breathe without using your voice, but you can never use your voice without the help of breath.

Breathing is so much more than simply pushing air in and out of our lungs; our very life depends on the rhythm of that breath. And everything that we need to do for a good voice has a lot to do with good, deep breathing. So, what is deep breathing?

In order to understand deep breathing, I would want you to know about the anatomy of voice production. Here is a brief explanation of how it all begins with a breath and emerges as words.

THE MECHANICS OF VOICE PRODUCTION

The wonderful sound we call voice is a result of complex interaction between various parts of our body. These include the lungs, the ribcage, the larynx (voice box), throat, mouth and nose.

Larynx

The larynx or voice box consists of ligaments, muscles and vocal cords. It is situated in the throat; part of it is the Adam's apple. It is not a rigid structure and it can move up and down in the neck. Hence, singers can vary the quality of their voices by pushing the voice box up and down in the neck. The exhaled air that emerges from the lungs vibrates the vocal cords and produces a sound – our voice. This voice gets resonance or tone in the cavity above the larynx or throat, and words are articulated in the oral cavity or mouth.

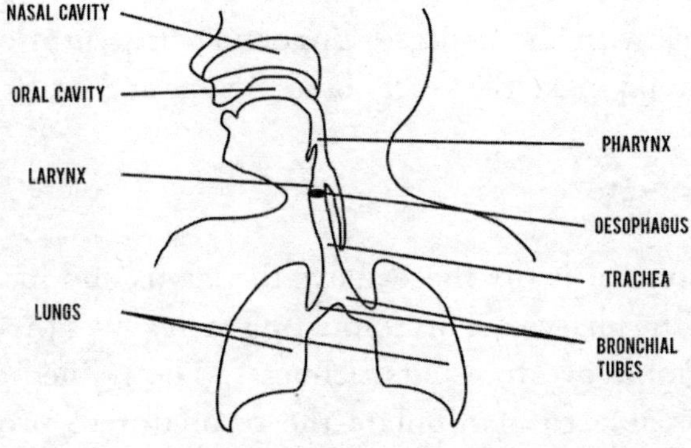

FIGURE 3.1: The vocal tract

We can roughly divide the production of voice into the following components:

The Generator

The generator is comprised of a pair of lungs that provides breath support. A regulated breath stream is the principal force that drives the vibration of the vocal folds. Without air flow through the larynx, the vocal folds can make no sound. Thus, the condition of the lungs and how efficiently the breath stream is utilized are the basic elements that influence one's vocal function.

The Vibrator

The larynx is the vibrator, specifically the fragile layers within the larynx called the vocal folds. Although the sound itself is produced in this organ, the richness and subtleties of articulation are the result of the sound and air moving through the resonator and articulators above the larynx. Problems with the delicate supporting structures of the larynx could make the voice sound hoarse and gruff.

The Resonator

The resonator is the space above the larynx and includes most of the pharynx. This resonating cavity gives the voice its harmonic overtones, its richness. (The trained opera singer is able to manipulate the resonator to produce resonance at 2,500 Hz, which allows the singer's voice to be heard above an entire orchestra.) Problems with the resonator are uncommon and although a tonsillectomy, for example, may cause a temporary setback, complete recovery is fairly quick.

The Articulator

The articulator is made up of the tongue, lips, cheeks, teeth and palate. These organs shape the sound from below into words and other vocal gestures. Medical problems involving the articulator are rare; for the singer, most issues with the articulator can be corrected by the voice coach or teacher.

Figure 3.2 shows a view of the vocal cords in action:

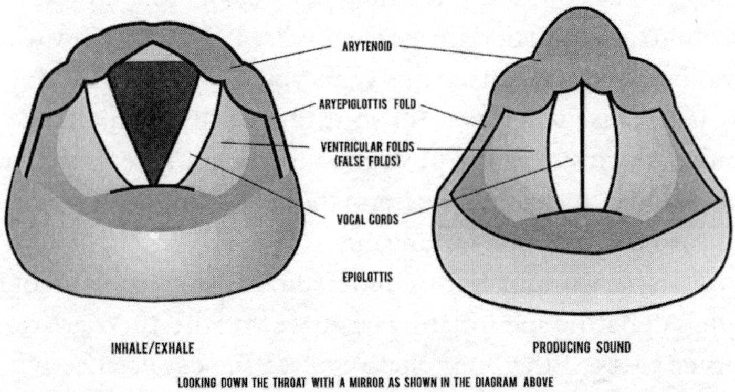

Figure 3.2: Vocal cords, open and closed

Deep Breathing

Let us try and understand deep breathing now. In simple terms, it means to fill your lungs with air. You might immediately ask me, 'Am I not doing this every minute?' Yes, you are breathing, but not always deep enough. Let us test it out and you can see for yourself what I am saying. Do this simple exercise.

Sit in a quiet place, close your eyes and pay attention to your breathing. While breathing, if your belly distends during inhalations, you are doing deep breathing. If only your chest is expanding and contracting without much movement of your abdomen or belly, you are definitely not breathing deep. Have you ever watched babies breathe while they are asleep? If you did, you may have observed that their belly goes up and down quite a bit. That is because they are doing deep breathing. And that is also the reason they can cry out loud, for long periods of time and don't seem to get tired or damage their voices. Do you know why the belly moves outwards, when you do deep breathing? It is because when you fill your lungs fully with air, they move downwards and push the diaphragm (the muscular partition between the chest and the abdomen) down, which in turn pushes your tummy out.

It is very important to understand that apart from our lungs deflating and inflating when we breathe, there are two other parts of the body that regulate the external activity of breathing. These are the ribcage and the abdomen. When you breathe deeply, the internal muscles of the diaphragm cause it to move downwards and force the belly to move outward. However, this alone is not enough. The movement of the ribcage is also needed to ensure the upper areas of the lungs are oxygenated as well. There are lots of techniques available for deep breathing, but getting it right is important. Therefore, if a technique involves minimal chest movement and focuses purely on belly distension, it is not good enough. We must develop a breathing technique which combines the movement of both, the ribcage and the belly. Only then will the entire lungs be filled with air. This is necessary to get a strong, robust and athletic voice.

One of my clients, a singer, was experiencing tremendous tension in her upper chest area and also complained of dizziness, especially while singing loudly and powerfully. She was pushing the diaphragm too forcefully and creating a tension in the chest area. This resulted in all the blood flowing into the chest, leaving her light-headed and exhausted. As soon as I taught her to use the chest and the belly in tandem, this problem disappeared. The idea here is to use all your chest and abdominal muscles to power your voice, not just the chest or the abdomen alone.

EXERCISES TO DEVELOP DEEP BREATHING

Here is a step-by-step guide to develop the ability to breathe deeply:

- Get yourself into a quiet space. Switch off your phones.
- Lie down on your back with your head supported by a pillow and your spine as evenly aligned with the head as possible. Alternatively, you may sit cross-legged and erect. Please ensure that you are wearing loose-fitting clothes that will allow your abdomen to move.
- Put one hand on your abdomen and the other on your chest.

- Inhale slowly, drawing in as much air as you possibly can until you are filled to capacity. You will notice that your chest and your belly bulge outwards.
- Now slowly exhale and observe your chest and belly constrict.
- Ensure that your shoulders are relaxed and still.
- The movement of the abdomen should be forward towards the sky and then back, and not upwards towards the head and then back down.
- When you have completed one cycle of respiration (inhalation and exhalation), breathe in again for the next.
- Do this for twelve counts before you take a break.
- Repeat the set of twelve deep breaths two more times.
- With time, you will be able to spontaneously take in more air with every breath.

Remember also that good breath control for a performance begins with a relaxed body. Tense muscles in the neck, tongue, jaw and throat constrict the vocal cords and cause the pitch of your voice to rise. Furthermore, tension in other parts of your body impairs the quality of your voice and undermines your ability to perform well. Relaxation and warm-up exercises will help you here. (Refer to the chapter titled 'The Complete Vocal Exercise Guide'.)

Tension, fear, stress and anxiety can all result in your breath getting caught in the chest or the throat, causing your voice to sound weak, shaky and unnatural. Breathing from your diaphragm provides greater power to your voice, allows you to perform for longer periods and also speak complex dialogues effortlessly.

Good breath control is what will finally make the difference between an actor being able to successfully deliver dialogues versus collapsing exhausted on the studio floor. An actor ought to be able to deal with the complex demands of voice and voice modulation, with sentences that never seem to end, often involving the hysterical histrionics of a given role, and he also has to make it all sound natural.

TRY THIS!

Read the following paragraph with lots of power in your voice and modulation:

'Meera, you cannot compel someone to feel love and affection for you. It can only be earned. Your constant coercion is suffocating me and if anything, it's actually pushing me further away from you. So, just relax and leave me alone!'

So, how did you do? If you made it all the way through without running out of air, congratulations. However, if you were gasping for breath towards the end, you need to increase your lung capacity and breath support.

Benefits of using your breath:

- Strong and powerful voice
- Ability to project your voice
- Flexibility of voice
- Endurance of voice
- Better capacity to emote
- Better control of voice

- Easy to modulate your voice
- Protection from voice damage
- Better tone of voice

Now that you have mastered the art of deep breathing, you have to learn the art of coordinating your breathing with your speech.

Breathing is also related to loudness which again we will discuss later in chapters five and nine. But just to get an idea, keep in mind that if you want to be loud you need to expel more air and when soft, less.

In conclusion, remember that mastering your breathing is the most important step towards developing a great voice. Therefore, BREATHE.

4

LEARNING TO SPEAK FROM THE BELLY, NOT FROM THE THROAT

Effective Use of the Voice

Now that you have learnt the art of deep breathing in isolation, the next step is to master the technique of harnessing the breath for voice production in your chosen profession, be it acting, singing, anchoring or teaching. The transition from the ability to breathe deep to using it in voicing is the most important lesson you will need to learn.

As your capacity for air intake increases, another key skill to develop is an awareness of precisely how much air you would need for a particular sentence. In other words, ensuring that you know the amount of air to inhale, that is, sufficient air for articulating the sentence before you. We all do this instinctively in normal conversations. If you need to say only a few words, you take in less air, and when you are planning a long sentence, you take a deeper breath.

The second thing to remember is to breathe in during normal pauses like commas and full stops and to breathe in when the other person is speaking. If you are delivering a speech or working on voicing a script or song, it makes sense to mark out, beforehand, the places where you need to breathe in. Over a period of time, as your breathing technique gets stronger, you will be inhaling enough air during the natural pauses. As the whole process becomes your second nature, you won't need reminders to inhale at the strategic places in your elocution, recitation or singing. In order to achieve that level of intuitive aspiration, you will need to practise the following steps.

FIRST WEEK

- Start by doing your deep breathing exercise.
- Sit cross-legged and wear loose-fitting clothes.
- Place one hand on your chest, the other on your lower abdomen.
- Take a deep breath. As you do that, you should be able to feel your stomach inflate.
- The shoulders and chest should remain still, the breathing soundless and you should be completely relaxed.
- As you breathe out, your stomach should deflate fully.
- This is one deep breath.
- Don't stop. Take the next breath without a break.
- Repeat this exercise twelve times.
- Now, take a break; then, do two more sets.

- Do this exercise twice or thrice every day.
- Also, become aware of your breathing throughout the day and consciously make it deeper.

SECOND WEEK

- Once you have learnt the above exercise to make your breathing deeper, let's try and use it for speech.
- Take a deep breath and then, as you exhale, say the vowel 'aa' as long as the breath lasts.
- Repeat the process with vowels 'ee' and 'oo'.
- Now, take a deep breath and start counting from one onwards. Say as many numbers as you can in a single breath. Repeat until you are able to count up to one hundred in one breath.
- The best way to determine whether you are using your breath and speaking from the stomach, not your throat, is if you can increase your voice volume comfortably – that is, without hurting your throat or larynx.

THIRD WEEK

- Now use the same number technique for reading.
- Take a deep breath and read aloud from a book or a newspaper, as many words as possible, for as long as the breath lasts.
- Stop; then, take another breath and continue.
- Repeat this exercise until you complete reading four to five pages (approximately 2,000 words).

FOURTH WEEK

- Continue reading, but breathe at the natural pauses – the full stops, the commas, the semicolons and the colons.
- This way you have learnt to read aloud by speaking from the abdomen and not from the throat.

Having learnt to breathe effectively and to use that while voicing, you have mastered the most important task in getting a great voice. However, there are a few more concepts you need to work on. So, let us go to the next chapter, which takes a look at the parameters of voice.

5

HOW TO GET THAT LOUD, BOOMING, RESONANT VOICE

Raise the Energy

Every actor aspires to have a resonant and powerful voice like Amrish Puri, Amitabh Bachchan and many others who are blessed with deep, commanding voices. I am fairly sure that in your quest for a booming baritone, you may have already come across various methodologies and quick-fix solutions by which you could achieve this end. While some methods might be right, others may just have been plain bizarre. You were probably even told that a rich, mellifluous voice is a God-given gift and if you don't have it, well ... you don't ... and it's well-nigh impossible to acquire. Right?

Let me explain. A booming voice is basically a loud voice. A resonant voice means one with a lot of tone and timbre. Basically, we are talking about a strong, commanding voice.

Yes, it is true that if you are naturally blessed with one, that's great. However, if you are not, there is nothing to worry about. You can develop one for sure.

Let's try and understand some basic concepts about the quality of voice here. The voice has three parameters.

1. Loudness
2. Pitch
3. Resonance

LOUDNESS

Loudness is easy to understand. It is the volume of your voice and you can go either loud or soft. But, is it as simple as that? Not really, because controlling the decibel levels of one's own voice at will is a challenge, and not always an easy task. How does one develop a loud voice? Basically, it is all about harnessing your breathing capacity. In order to sound loud you need to expel more air. In the earlier chapter, we discussed learning to breathe deeply and the ways and means to incorporate deep breathing into your speech. Taking that technique forward, you need to learn to exhale with force but effortlessly. This form of exhalation will need to be maintained throughout your speech or song in order to be really loud.

Therefore, every time you speak you need to be breathing properly and also using the breath to amplify your voice.

PITCH

Let's understand pitch. Pitch is the frequency of your voice. What is meant by frequency? Frequency is the number of times your vocal cords vibrate in one second. Is that too technical to understand? Let me explain in a much simpler way. Amitabh Bachchan has a low-pitched voice while Lata Mangeshkar has a high-pitched voice. Now you have a basic understanding of what pitch is. Nonetheless, there is a lot more you need to know. The pitch of your voice is determined by the length and thickness of your vocal cords. Technically, since the length and thickness of your vocal cords can't change, it automatically implies that you can't change your pitch. However, with some guidance, these cords can be trained and you can learn to adjust the frequency of your voice to take the pitch a notch higher or lower. The vocal cords are elastic in nature and hence can be elongated to a small extent. Furthermore, one can learn to vibrate only the upper portion or the lower, thereby reducing the length of the vibrating section, which in turn alters the pitch. Therefore, for a higher pitch, control the lower segment of the vocal cords to keep it stationary and allow only the upper part to vibrate. For a lower pitch, increase the length of the vocal cords by stretching them slightly, and voila, you've got yourself a deep bass.

How is the pitch of your voice related to a resonant, booming and powerful voice? Well, your voice will sound loudest in your natural pitch. If you raise or lower the pitch from its natural frequency, it will reduce the volume. Let me explain this with a graph (Figure 5.1).

So, as you can see from the figure, the voice is at its most stentorious at the middle of the curve, which is your natural pitch, and when you move away from your natural pitch, going either lower or higher, the volume diminishes.

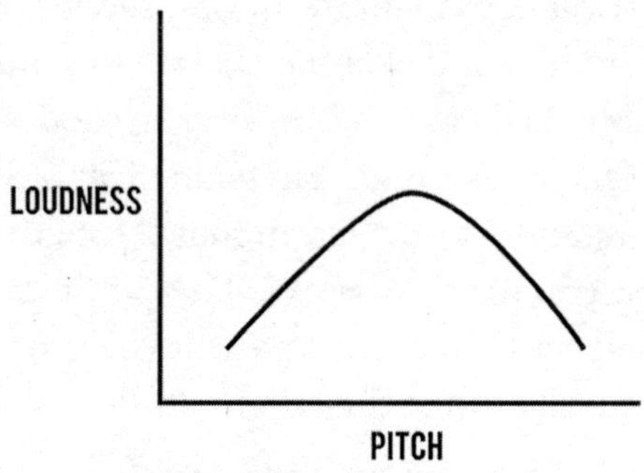

FIGURE 5.1: Loudness and pitch bell curve

Therefore, for that loud, powerful voice you need to breathe deeply, use the ejected exhalation as you speak and also stay as close as possible to your natural pitch.

RESONANCE

What is resonance?

Resonance is similar to an echo. The empty spaces above the voice box in the throat, the mouth, the nose and sinuses act as natural echo chambers. The voice gets a lot of tone, timbre and texture from reverberations within these cavities. Exercises to improve resonance can work wonders.

There are three types of resonance:

- The first is the pharyngeal or throat resonance, where the air basically vibrates in the throat area. Sounds like 'ha' tend to use throat resonance. Place your hand on the throat and say 'ha-ha', you can feel the vibration.
- The second resonance is the oral or mouth resonance, where the air ricochets within the oral cavity. Sounds

like 'pa', 'la', 'ka', 'va', 'fa', 'tha' and 'ta' are all essentially mouth resonances.

- The third is the nasal resonance where the sound thrums within the nasal passages and sinuses. Sounds like 'ma' and 'na' have a natural nasal resonance.

When we speak, we use all three resonances, predominantly the mouth or oral resonance. You can learn to speak well in all the three resonances with training and thus produce different types of voices.

All in all, in order to acquire that booming, resonant and powerful voice, you need to breathe in deeply, exhale strongly, use your natural pitch and predominantly use mouth resonance with effective nasal and throat resonances where required.

The following curves (Figures 5.2 and 5.3) show the relationship between loudness and resonance, and pitch and resonance, respectively.

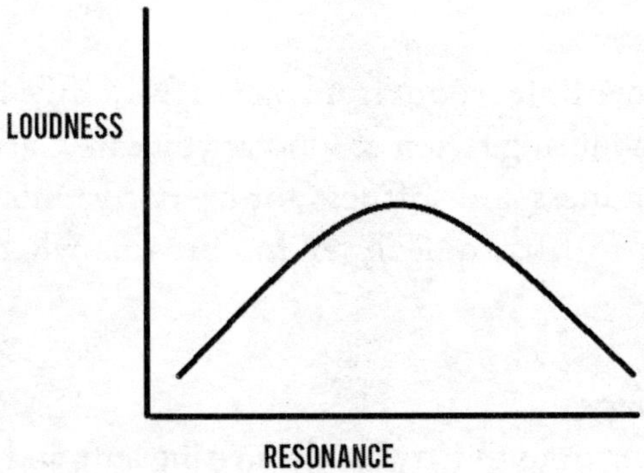

FIGURE 5.2: Relationship between loudness and resonance

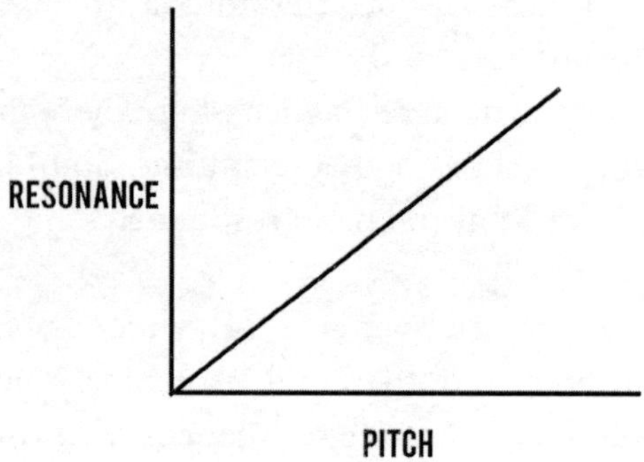

FIGURE 5.3: Relationship between pitch and resonance

Here are some exercises to boost the parameters of your voice, improve its flexibility and also aid in vocal modulation.

WEEKS ONE AND TWO

Loudness Exercises

Mastering the extremes

Take a deep breath and count from one to five softly. From six, continue counting to ten as loud as you can. Carry on alternating loudness and softness for every five numbers and count up to fifty, quickly taking breaths whenever needed.

Alternating loudness

Say the numbers one to fifty by alternating soft and loud for each number. Therefore, you whisper 'one', shout out 'two', whisper 'three', a loud 'four' and so on, taking quick breaths as required.

The train

Say the numbers one to fifty starting with a very soft voice, gradually increasing volume until you reach your maximum decibel level. Repeat the procedure, this time begin at your loudest and gradually decrease the volume until you arrive at a whisper. Take quick breaths when required.

Pitch Exercises

Mastering the extremes

Take a deep breath and count from one to five in a low pitch and six to ten in a high pitch. Continue alternating pitch, high and low, for every five numbers up to fifty, inhaling quickly whenever needed.

Alternating pitch

Count from one to fifty by alternating low and high pitch for each number. Therefore, you say a deep-voiced 'one', a shrill 'two', a bass 'three', a squeaky 'four' and so on, until you reach fifty. Inhale deeply and quickly as required.

The train

Count from one to fifty starting with a very low pitch and gradually increasing until you reach your maximum pitch. (Akin to doing the scales or 'sa re ga ma'.) And then repeat the process, but this time the pitch's gradient decreases with every count until you reach the lowest pitch. Remember to inhale quick, deep breaths whenever needed.

Resonance Exercises

- Count from one to fiftypredominantly using throat resonance – this produces a timbre in tone.
- Count from one to fifty predominantly using mouth or oral resonance – this sounds a lot like the voice of God in the movies, with an echo-like quality.
- Count from one to fifty predominantly using nasal resonance – with a twang as in a Texas accent.

In all three exercises, take quick, deep, breaths as required.

WEEK THREE

Read a newspaper or your script or presentation alternating soft and loud for each sentence. That is, read one sentence in a whisper, the next loudly and so on. Do the same with pitch and resonance. These exercises do not carry any obvious relevance in terms of modulation or punctuation, however, they go a long way to help increase the voice's flexibility and to modify the parameters of the natural voice.

Having learnt and mastered the parameters of voice, let us move on to another facet of vocal volume that also involves resonance and pitch – voice projection.

6

VOICE PROJECTION

Throwing Your Voice Around

Voice projection refers to the strength in your voice while speaking or singing. It not only refers to the voice's volume, it also pertains to the carrying quality that makes a voice heard over a distance, like that of a teacher who needs to be heard by backbenchers in a classroom. This aspect is very pertinent to a theatre actor where the voice conveys all the emotions and expressions to the audience in the last rows who lack the advantage of being able to see the thespian's minute facial expressions. The same is true for a lawyer who needs to reach out to the judge who is sometimes seated far away. Basically, this refers to a skill by which your voice travels over a good distance without the help of a microphone. This quality instantly captures the attention of the audience and is a brilliant technique used to command respect. So, whether you are speaking to a packed auditorium or conducting a presentation in a conference room, effective voice projection is imperative if you want people to hear you clearly and take you seriously as a speaker.

So, how is voice projection done? Voice projection is directly related to the amount of air you exhale. Normally, when we speak, we do expel air. However, if you want your voice to be really loud and heard across a great expanse, you need to expel more air and you will have to do it very quickly. Therefore, if you think of the expelled air as fuel for voice projection, you need a quick burst of air in a large quantity. So, in normal speech, if a lungful of air allows you to say three to four sentences, a projected voice will be able to say only two or three words with the same amount of air. Often, during normal speech, we use air from the top of our lungs, and quickly replenish that in every natural pause, without actually depleting the entire stock of air in the lungs. However, when you project your voice, the entire lung is evacuated of air in a short span of time. Therefore, the deep-breathing technique is the backbone for voice projection. In addition to using a lungful of air, you will also need to relax all the muscles involved. Tension in the muscles hampers swift and complete exhalation. Hence, a good vocal technique, a well-balanced respiration method and a relaxed larynx are crucial for effective voice projection.

The following are the four essentials to the art of voice projection:

- Breathing technique
- Resonance

- Pitch
- Posture

BREATHING TECHNIQUE

As mentioned earlier, good voice projection requires efficient working of the lungs, intercostal muscles and diaphragm. Basically, the diaphragm helps to eject air in a short span of time in strong gusts. When the diaphragm fills with air it pushes downward, the belly distends and when you breathe out, the abdomen tautens, the diaphragm rises and expels the air. Deep breathing exercises help strengthen the infrastructure of the body's respiratory apparatus and thereby have a positive impact on one's voice production mechanisms.

RESONANCE

The resonators are echo chambers around the larynx. They are like speakers in your vocal system, so the voice that originates from the vocal cords reverberates through the throat, the mouth and the nose and each resonator imbues a special quality to the sound produced. For example, a person could have a nasal twang when the echo chambers of the nose are brought into play, or a guttural timbre when the sound is produced through the throat, and so on. Hence, voice projection involves opening up of the throat and the oral cavity. Imagine if you spoke without opening your mouth much. Such speech would be barely audible – a mumble, mutter or a whisper at best. One needs to exert concentrated pressure as sound passes through the resonating chambers of the mouth and nose in order to produce projection. A strong reverberation in these echo chambers around the larynx will produce the greatest projection available to your voice by utilizing all the key resonators of throat, mouth and nose.

PITCH

Everyone has an optimal pitch and unless you speak at your ideal pitch, you will not have the required loudness or projection. As mentioned in the previous chapter, the decibel level of the voice is related to resonance and pitch. Therefore, the loudest volume would be possible in your natural pitch, using oral resonance (rather than the nasal passages or throat).

POSTURE

An upright posture is required for good voice projection as it will allow your lungs and diaphragm to move optimally and also help to open up your resonators. Furthermore, this position reduces tension in the neck muscles. Avoid slouching or leaning forward. Sitting upright or standing up straight are the best stances for optimum voice projection.

To summarize, if you need to project your voice, have an erect posture, use a good diaphragmatic breathing technique, relax the muscles, open the throat and mouth (like a yawn) and use your natural pitch.

EXERCISES

Week One

- Relaxation exercises (yawn, sigh). When we yawn and sigh, our muscles naturally go into a relaxed state. Hence we use this to achieve relaxation of all vocal muscles. Do the following exercise. Take a deep breath in and as you breathe out, yawn. In the next breath, breathe in and sigh as you breathe out. Alternate yawn and sigh for twenty breaths. This will relax all your muscles.
- Take a deep breath and say one vowel loudly per breath. Remember that you are not shouting or screaming but saying it in a very strong voice, from your belly and not from your throat. So, basically you are creating a contrast between your soft, conversational voice and a loud, booming, resonant voice. Imagine a wire extending from your mouth to the corner of the room and project your voice along this line.

Week Two

Repeat exercises one and two of week one, and then:

- Take a deep breath and project your voice as you say the numbers – three numbers per breath.
- Single words: take a deep breath and use a single breath to project a single word. You could use a dictionary for a list of words.
- If you have mastered the word level, use short phrases. Take a deep breath and project an entire phrase.

All that you have learnt so far about voice is like the foundation of a building which is essential to uphold the edifice of speech. We use speech for communication and speech is expressed through voice. Let us examine some aspects of speech that you need to work on in the next chapter on diction.

7

DICTION

The Science of Sounds

Diction, also known as pronunciation skills, is something that has been drilled into each one of us right from our school days. Having good pronunciation with clear enunciation is always an asset in communication skills, especially if you are using your voice and speech for your profession, be that of an actor, a singer or a corporate professional.

Let me make one point clear – diction is not language-specific. Diction is about sounds. And sounds are the same in all languages. Having said that, there is an aspect of diction which is language-specific; in other words, the combination in which we use the sounds varies from language to language; sometimes these combinations can be difficult or tricky for us to pronounce. We shall talk about the combinations a bit later. For now, let us get back to the basics.

There are three aspects of pronunciation or articulation. The voice is produced by the vocal cords, gathering tone, timbre, resonance and volume as the sound moves up the throat. This basic voice is then moulded into distinct sounds by the movements of our tongue, palate, teeth, lips and jaws. Basically, the air that you breathe out is constricted and then released to produce a variety of sounds. Depending on the precise sound you want to produce, the relevant parts of your mouth, tongue, teeth, etc., constrict and shape the sound which emerges. This is called the place of articulation. For example, if we want to say the sound 'pa' we press our lips together and constrict the air behind it before parting the lips to produce the sound. There are different kinds of constriction, some complete and some partial (which is called manner of articulation). There are also sounds in which we vibrate the vocal cords a little more than we do for normal voicing.

I shall briefly talk here about phonetics, although it is not within the purview of this book to go into too many details. The science of sound production is called phonetics. Sounds, as many of you must be aware, can be divided into vowels and consonants. When we use vowels, there is minimal or no restriction of the air that you breathe out; all constricted air exhalation occurs during enunciating the consonants.

Let me explain a few significant concepts of consonants.

VIBRATION OF VOCAL CORD CLASSIFICATION

Consonants are divided into voiced and voiceless (or

unvoiced) sounds depending on the vibrations of the vocal cords. Voiced sounds are those in which there is a full vibration of the vocal cords. Examples of such sounds are 'bha', 'dha', 'gha', 'za' and so on. The voiceless sounds, on the other hand, do not have any vibration of the vocal cords, examples of which are 'pa' or 'sa'.

An important point that I'd like to mention here is that the sound, be it voiced or unvoiced, has little or no bearing on diction. Whereas the next two aspects of diction that we are going to discuss – place of articulation and manner of articulation – are the key factors to develop excellent pronunciation skills.

PLACE OF ARTICULATION

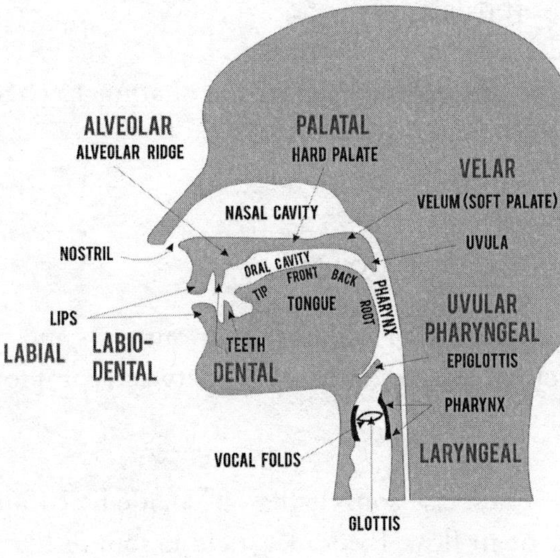

FIGURE 7.1: Place of articulation

Speech sounds are classified by the part of your mouth used in making the sound. Here is the basic classification:

- Bilabial: Sound made using both lips to constrict the air
  Examples: 'p' as in pat, 'b' as in bat
- Labiodental: Sound made using the lower lip and upper teeth to constrict the air
  Examples: 'f' as in fat, 'v' as in vase
- Alveolar: Sound made where the tongue touches the alveolar ridge to compress the air
  Examples: 'd' as in dad, 's' as in sat
- Dental: Sound made using the teeth and tongue
  Example: 'th' as in the
- Velar: Sound made using the back part of the tongue and the soft palate
  Examples: 'k' as in cat, 'g' as in gate
- Pharyngeal: Sound made using the pharynx to channel the breath
  Example: 'h' as in have

MANNER OF ARTICULATION

Manner of articulation is about the various ways and types of air restriction, i.e., the entire range between complete to lax or minimal closure.

- Plosives: These are sounds that are made by complete stoppage of air flow. Examples include sounds like 'pa', 'ba', 'ta', 'da', 'ka' and 'ga'.

- Nasal: Sounds that are made when air escapes through the nasal cavity. The examples of these are 'ma' and 'na'.
- Fricative: a sound produced by near-complete stoppage of air. The examples of this are 'sa', 'za', 'fa' and 'va'.
- Approximant: the sound made where one articulator (part of mouth) comes close to another without touching and without causing audible friction. The examples of this are 'wa', 'ra' and 'la'.
- Affricate: a sound that begins with complete closure and is released with minimal closure. Examples include 'sh'.

Therefore, in order to achieve perfect diction, one has to learn to move one's tongue, lips and palate in the various degrees of closure at various junctures. When we speak words and sentences, this is done as a continuous stream with perfect coordination of the various parts of the mouth. Ergo, achieving perfect diction requires a great deal of practice.

Words are combinations of vowels and consonants which are language-specific. Certain languages have certain key combinations which form the identity of the language. So, depending on the language which you use for your profession, you will have to work on specific diction skills. For example, in Hindi, the distinction between the voiced and voiceless is very significant, at times it can change the meaning of the word altogether. For instance, consider the sounds 'ka' and 'kha'. So, 'kaan' means ear, while 'khaan' means a mine (as in coal mine). In Tamil, as there is no demarcation such as voiced or unvoiced at all, there is only 'ka' and no 'kha'.

Not all languages are phonetic. That is, quite often the spelling and the pronunciation of the words don't synchronize. The English language is a good example of this. So, when one wants to perfect the diction of such languages, it is more difficult and one needs a proper coach for guidance in order to get an in-depth knowledge of the language. However, most Indian languages, like Hindi and Marathi are phonetic languages – the written sounds and the pronounced sounds are the same. Therefore, mastering the diction of such languages is a lot easier. For this specific reason, I wish to make an important suggestion here that if your line of work involves speaking in any of the Indian languages, try and learn the script of that Indian language because by transcribing the material into the Roman script you will lose the advantage of the phonetic ease of the original language. For example, if a paragraph in Hindi is converted into Roman (English), the accent will sound anglicized and erroneous; whereas if it is written in Hindi (Devanagari script), which is a phonetic language unlike English and corresponds exactly with phonation, one would not mispronounce words for Hindi elocution.

Words are a combination of vowels and consonants. For example, the word 'cat' starts with a consonant 'c', followed by the vowel 'a' and ends with a consonant 't'. These are simple words. All languages have certain combination sounds. Sometimes you have two vowels coming together. For example, the sound 'ou', as in stout, is a combination of 'o' and 'u'. These are called diphthongs. These are more difficult to pronounce. There could be a combination of consonants as well, like 'st', 'tr', 'sk', 'ksh' and so on, without a vowel in between. Again, these require a little more practice. Certain words have several combination sounds in them – for example, the Hindi word 'akasmaat' meaning 'suddenly'. Therefore, diction is not just about the sounds or the words, it encompasses the deeper understanding of language-specific combinations. Furthermore, it clearly demonstrates that there are no shortcuts to long hours of rote practice to acquire perfect diction.

Having discussed the science of sounds and about its application in various languages, it is time I gave you a few tips on perfecting your diction. For starters, I am listing down the phonetic charts for Hindi and English here (Figure 7.2 and 7.3). One can easily acquire and use the phonetic chart of any language from the school books of that language. These charts are also plentiful on the Internet.

	monophthongs				diphthongs			
VOWELS	i: sheep	ɪ ship	ʊ good	u: shoot	ɪə here	eɪ wait		voiced unvoiced
	e bed	ə teacher	ɜ: bird	ɔ: door	ʊə tourist	ɔɪ boy	əʊ show	
	æ cat	ʌ up	ɑ: far	ɒ on	eə hair	aɪ my	aʊ cow	
CONSONANTS	p pea	b boat	t tea	d dog	ʧ cheese	ʤ June	k car	g go
	f fly	v video	θ think	ð this	s see	z zoo	ʃ shall	ʒ television
	m man	n now	ŋ sing	h hat	l love	r red	w wet	j yes

FIGURE 7.2: Phonetic chart (English)

क	का	कि	की	कृ	कू	के	कै	को	कौ	कं	कः
ख	खा	खि	खी	खृ	खू	खे	खै	खो	खौ	खं	खः
ग	गा	गि	गी	गृ	गू	गे	गै	गो	गौ	गं	गः
घ	घा	घि	घी	घृ	घू	घे	घै	घो	घौ	घं	घः
ङ	ङा	ङि	ङी	ङृ	ङू	ङे	ङै	ङो	ङौ	ङं	ङः
च	चा	चि	ची	चृ	चू	चे	चै	चो	चौ	चं	चः
छ	छा	छि	छी	छृ	छू	छे	छै	छो	छौ	छं	छः
ज	जा	जि	जी	जृ	जू	जे	जै	जो	जौ	जं	जः
झ	झा	झि	झी	झृ	झू	झे	झै	झो	झौ	झं	झः
ट	टा	टि	टी	टृ	टू	टे	टै	टो	टौ	टं	टः
ठ	ठा	ठि	ठी	ठृ	ठू	ठे	ठै	ठो	ठौ	ठं	ठः
ड	डा	डि	डी	डृ	डू	डे	डै	डो	डौ	डं	डः
ढ	ढा	ढि	ढी	ढृ	ढू	ढे	ढै	ढो	ढौ	ढं	ढः
ण	णा	णि	णी	णृ	णू	णे	णै	णो	णौ	णं	णः
त	ता	ति	ती	तृ	तू	ते	तै	तो	तौ	तं	तः
थ	था	थि	थी	थृ	थू	थे	थै	थो	थौ	थं	थः
द	दा	दि	दी	दृ	दू	दे	दै	दो	दौ	दं	दः
ध	धा	धि	धी	धृ	धू	धे	धै	धो	धौ	धं	धः
न	ना	नि	नी	नृ	नू	ने	नै	नो	नौ	नं	नः
प	पा	पि	पी	पृ	पू	पे	पै	पो	पौ	पं	पः
फ	फा	फि	फी	फृ	फू	फे	फै	फो	फौ	फं	फः
य	या	यि	यी	यृ	यू	ये	यै	यो	यौ	यं	यः
भ	भा	भि	भी	भृ	भू	भे	भै	भो	भौ	भं	भः
म	मा	मि	मी	मृ	मू	मे	मै	मो	मौ	मं	मः
य	या	यि	यी	यृ	यू	ये	य	यो	यौ	यं	यः
र	रा	रि	री	रृ	रू	रे	रै	रो	रौ	रं	रः
ल	ला	लि	ली	लृ	लू	ले	लै	लो	लौ	लं	लः
व	वा	वि	वी	वृ	वू	वे	व	वो	वौ	वं	वः
श	शा	शि	शी	शृ	शू	शे	शै	शो	शौ	शं	शः
ष	षा	षि	षी	षृ	षू	षे	षै	षो	षौ	षं	षः
स	सा	सि	सी	सृ	सू	से	सै	सो	सौ	सं	सः
ह	हा	हि	ही	हृ	हू	हे	है	हो	हौ	हं	हः
क्ष	क्षा	क्षि	क्षी	क्षृ	क्षू	क्षे	क्षै	क्षो	क्षौ	क्षं	क्षः
त्र	त्रा	त्रि	त्री	त्रृ	त्रू	त्रे	त्रै	त्रो	त्रौ	त्रं	त्रः
ज्ञ	ज्ञा	ज्ञि	ज्ञी	ज्ञृ	ज्ञू	ज्ञे	ज्ञै	ज्ञो	ज्ञौ	ज्ञं	ज्ञः

FIGURE 7.3: Phonetic chart (Hindi)

EXERCISES FOR DICTION

Part One

Since diction calls for flexibility of the tongue, lips, palate, etc., start off by performing simple tongue and lip exercises.

Part Two

- Read the phonetic chart. How do you know you are reading it right? This is one section where you will need verbal guidance from either a teacher or online recordings. As soon as you have mastered the correct pronunciation of each sound, move to the next step.
- Make a list of words with each sound in the beginning of a word, middle of a word and end of a word. Can you guess where you can find such a perfect list? Of course, the dictionary of that particular language! So, start reading the dictionary. The dictionary of any language is the best collection of words with all possible sounds and all possible sound combinations.
- When you have mastered the pronunciation of all sounds at word level, move on to sentence level. Read aloud from any reading material like a book or a newspaper, keeping in mind the proper pronunciation of all words.
- Make a list of combination sounds. For example, 'st', 'tr', 'ksh', etc. Practise them at the sound and word levels before moving on to the sentence level. The dictionary is the best place to find all the available combinations in that language.
- The moment you feel that you have done enough practice, it might be a good idea to record your reading and listen to yourself. Ask your teacher, if you have one, or a trusted friend, to check on your pronunciation.
- As soon as you feel you have developed a fairly good diction of the language, you can practise tongue-twisters

which will test your pronunciation skills. Here is a small list of tongue-twisters in Hindi and in English.

ENGLISH TONGUE-TWISTERS

- Six sick hicks nick six slick bricks with picks and sticks.
- Picky people pick Peter Pan Peanut Butter; 'tis the peanut butter picky people pick.
- There those thousand thinkers were thinking, 'How did the other three thieves go through?'
- How much pot could a pot-roast roast, if a pot-roast could roast pot?
- Mr Tongue Twister tried to train his tongue to twist and turn and twit and twat to learn the letter 'T'.
- She saw Sheriff's shoes on the sofa. But was she so sure she saw Sheriff's shoes on the sofa?
- The Smothers brothers' father's mother's brothers are the Smothers brothers' mother's father's other brothers.
- I slit the sheet, the sheet I slit, and on the slit sheet I sit.
- Six slippery snails slid slowly seaward.
- Gertie's great-grandma grew aghast at Gertie's grammar.
- Imagine an imaginary menagerie manager managing an imaginary menagerie.
- The thirty-three thieves thought that they thrilled the throne throughout Thursday.
- Silly Simon's sitting in a shoeshine shop. When he sits, he shines, and when he shines, he sits.

- A good cook could cook as much cookies as a good cook who could cook cookies.
- Did Dick Pickens prick his pinkie pickling cheap cling peaches in an inch of pinch or framing his famed French finch photos?
- Who washed Washington's white woollen underwear when Washington's weather woman went West?

HINDI TONGUE-TWISTERS

- Madan Mohan Malviya Madras mein machhli maarte maarte mare.
- Chaar Kachari Kachche Chacha,
Chaar Kachari Pakke.
Pakki Kachari Kachche Chacha,
Kachchi Kachari Pakke!
- Raja Gope Gopal Gopaggam Daas.
- Khadak Singh ke khadakne se khadakti hain khidkiyan, khidkiyon ke khadakne se khadakta hai Khadak Singh.
- Chandu ke chacha ne chandu ki chachi ko Chandni Chowk mein chaandi ki chammach se chatni chackayi.
- Samajh samajh ke samajh ko samjho.
Samajh samajh ke samajh ko samajhna hi samajh hai.
Jo samajh ko samajh kar bhi na samjhe
Voh kya hai? Nasamajh hai.
- Kaccha papad, pakka papad.
- Mar hum bhi gaye, marham ke liye, marham na mila.
Hum dum se gaye, humdum ke liye, humdum na mila.

DICTION ERRORS

What are some of the errors that one could commit? Pronunciation blunders are closely related to our next topic, 'Accents'. Diction and accent are first cousins. So, let's move on to our next topic.

8

ACCENTS

To Have It or Not?

We all understand accents, or that's what we like to think! When someone's speech has got a strong accent, we recognize it and remark, 'He's got an accent.' But what exactly does that mean?

DEFINITION

When you transpose the flavours or characteristics from one language into another, it is called an accent. There are a few exceptions to this rule – e.g., Cockney or Brogue – where the accent is more region-specific and is a distinct dialect. Most of these inflections are diction-oriented. Very few are from other aspects of speech. Let us discuss this a little bit more in detail.

In India, where there is such a rich variety of spoken languages and dialects, it is only natural that accent is given paramount importance. Although many of us speak English and Hindi, and at least some are probably schooled in English, there are so many different kinds of English that we get to hear. Most people, namely, those whose mother tongue is not Hindi, also speak their own mother tongues in addition to English and Hindi. Over the last four to five decades, a lot has changed and many of our youth are not very proficient in their mother tongue.

Most people between the age group of twenty to thirty are also world travellers, and they pick up myriad accents from overseas. This generation of young urban professionals has opportunities to learn to speak foreign languages like French, German, Spanish, Japanese and so on. Therefore, along with the vast array of Indian languages which could influence the Indian accent, the accents of the Western hemisphere and the Orient also feature in our linguistic landscape. A lot of how we speak depends on where and how we grew up. You've probably noticed that we tend to talk like the people with whom we spend most of our time in terms of vocabulary, terminology, pronunciation and accent. Therefore, our speech and diction is modelled on the way our parents, schoolfellows, associates and friends speak. Some schools are emphatically insistent upon proper articulation and pristine pronunciation, and if you happened to have attended one of those, you are probably blessed with excellent diction. If you did not, you need to put in a lot of work to consciously neutralize your accent.

In any case, the influence of the native language, which is spoken at home by our near and dear ones, is potent. As children, we have learnt to speak by listening to our parents and grandparents. Studies have shown that language skills are developed between the ages of zero and three years. By the end of this period, the child has become proficient in understanding and speaking the language. The learning process up to this time is entirely verbal, that is, the child learns the language only by listening and doing his best to relate everything to the various things in his young life. It is a learning that happens with no awareness, almost like the child is on autopilot. As a result, language is something that sinks into our subconscious mind and remains there lifelong. Because our native language is etched so deeply into our minds, we can never really forget it even if we speak it only once in a while and not very fluently at that. Its influence will always superimpose itself upon all the languages that we go on to speak later.

We usually don't realize we have an accent (intonations of our native tongue overlying our diction), unless other people point it out. This lack of self-awareness is the reason why correcting one's accent or diction is not an easy task. Frequently, we try to improve our pronunciation skills by listening to prominent speakers and imitating their diction. However, as we often realize, these efforts are futile. What one needs is an in-depth understanding of the problem and loads of practice in order to systematically overcome the issue.

Despite all this effort, when one is under stress or being inattentive, the old accent will tend to slip out – this is the aspect that one needs to work on diligently.

If you are going to be in a profession that expects you to speak impeccable Hindi or English, one needs to pay a lot of attention to eradicate and clean up inflections deeply entrenched in the subconscious. An objective examination of one's own speech (a recording, perhaps) will help identify the influence of other languages in it. It will take a lot of sustained effort and hard work to change old habits, because, at the end of the day, speaking in a particular way is a reflexive and intuitive habit developed since childhood. Self-help and self-awareness are needed to identify and correct the defects in your diction. Without self-awareness, you will not be able to recognize the pronunciation flaws that you need to work on. Moreover, with unbiased self-perception, one develops an instinctive recognition of the problem areas in one's speech. Recognizing and correcting the errors is merely the first hurdle to overcome. To translate it into fluent speech is the next step – a difficult step which may require professional help and many, many hours of dedicated practice.

It is often helpful to have someone else listening to you as you work on correcting your diction and accent. It could be a speech therapist, a voice coach or even a fellow professional who has some knowledge of proper diction and accents and can at least flag up your errors. Reading and correcting your accent with the help of this manual will not be the equivalent of getting yourself a live coach; however, your simpler speech issues can be addressed using this book. If you have some very hard-wired elocution handicaps, these will most certainly need professional help.

Now, let us examine some common accent and diction errors that you could be committing.

VOWEL REPLACEMENT

As we discussed in the chapter on diction, different languages use different sets of vowels from the common bank of possible vowels that a human being can produce. Some languages use a particular set of vowels more than the other sets. These become the hallmark of that language. Here are a few examples:

- In Marathi, the extended vowels are more frequently used than the shorter version of the vowel. Therefore, a person whose native language is Marathi tends to use this feature even in English. For example, he would say 'baaool' for bowl and 'Singaapore' for Singapore. Basically, he replaces the 'a' with 'aa'.
- The reverse happens in Punjabi where they tend to shorten a vowel rather than elongate it. For example, 'gaadi' which means a car in Hindi, becomes 'gadi'. But there are instances where they too stretch the vowels, so 'tension' becomes 'taension'. Therefore, unwittingly one could be elongating or truncating the vowels at all the wrong places. Hence, the idea is not about shortening or lengthening vowels indiscriminately, but to do so appropriately for the word.
- There could be instances of complete vowel replacements. For example, a Malayali speaking English would pronounce 'wrong' (which has an 'awe' sound phonetically) as 'rong' (replacing the 'awe' sound with an 'o'). A Tamil speaker would say 'wraang' (replacing the 'awe' with 'aa').

- In Bengali, again the vowels are elongated or even changed. So, 'beer' becomes 'bare'.
- The Kannada language has the tendency to shorten or replace vowels, and hence the word 'food' is pronounced as 'fud'. A long 'oo' becomes a short 'u'.

Since vowels are such an integral part of every word and our speech, vowel substitutions are the most difficult to correct and could require months of fastidious and diligent practice along with professional help.

CONSONANT REPLACEMENT

As we discussed in the chapter on diction, different languages use different sets of consonants from the common bank of possible consonants that a human being can produce. Some languages also use a particular set of consonants a lot more than all the other consonants present in the language. These become the hallmark of that language.

For example, in Marathi, the sound 'thcha' is a very commonly used consonant.

There are certain sounds in Indian languages which do not exist in the English phonetics or alphabets, and hence, it is not possible to use the English language to give examples. Therefore, when clients train with me, I can verbally explain these consonants to them. That, unfortunately, is beyond the purview of this book. However, I will share a few examples of consonant replacement here with you.

- In Parsi language, the following sounds do not exist: 'th' and 'dh'. Therefore, 'teeth' becomes 'teet', and 'Dhadhar' (the name of a suburb) becomes 'Dadar'. 'Father' and 'mother' are pronounced 'fadder' and 'mudder'.
- In Bengali, there is no 'v' sound. Therefore, when they speak any other language, all the 'v's in their words are substituted with 'b's or 'bh's. For instance, 'Vidya' becomes 'Bidya', victory becomes 'bhictory', and so on.
- In Tamil, we do not have the voiced counterpart for plosives, which means they have only 'pa', 'ba', 'ta', 'da', 'ka' and 'ga' and do not have 'pha', 'bha', 'tha', 'dha', 'kha' or 'gha'. Therefore, when a Tamil person speaks Hindi, they will say 'kaan' (which means ear) instead of 'khaan' (which means a mine – as in gold mine). Such substitutions may not always change the meaning of the words, but they make the language which is being spoken sound very odd and funny.
- In the languages of Tamil and Malayalam, the sibilants are more 'z' than 's', and often the 's' sounds get replaced by 'z'. For example, 'listened' becomes 'lizzened'.
- Another influence of Malayalam on English is the interchange of consonants. Hence, 'wanted' is often pronounced as 'wandet'.
- In the Hindi-speaking states also this swapping of alphabets is discernible. The word 'proposed' is pronounced as 'porposed'.

SYLLABIC BREAKS

Words are made up of syllables. A syllable contains a minimum of one vowel and one consonant, although there may be more. Words are made up of one or more syllables. Here are a few examples:

- The word 'water' has two syllables, the first being 'wa' and the second, 'ter'.
- The word 'book' has only one syllable.
- The word 'telephone' has three syllables – 'te', 'le' and 'phone'.

We pause between syllables for a fraction of a second when we pronounce words. The place to take the syllabic break is language-specific and is learnt by listening to the language as there are no rules for this. It is a learnt behaviour. Transference of syllabic breaks happens unconsciously when one switches languages. Here are a few examples:

- Predominantly Hindi-speaking persons break up long words in English rather differently. Instead of 'technology', it becomes 'tech-no-logy'. Or instead of 'physiology' it is pronounced 'phys-yo-logy'.
- In Tamil, the syllabic breaks are different. Hence, 'listened' is pronounced 'lis-ten-ed', instead of 'listened'.

OVEREMPHASIS OF PLOSIVE CONSONANTS AND TRILLS

Certain languages like Tamil and Malayalam have intrinsically more emphasis on the plosive consonants – that is, 'p', 'ph', 'b', 'bh', 't', 'th', 'd', 'dh', 'k', 'kh' and 'g', 'gh'. The same happens to the trill consonant 'ra'. Here are some examples:

- When south Indians speak Hindi words like 'paneer' (cottage cheese) they pronounce it as 'pannner'; the word 'chana' (chickpea) becomes 'channna'.
- Words in English like 'terrible' or 'horrible' become 'terrrible' or 'horrrible'.

DROPPING THE ENDS OF WORDS

People tend to drop the end of a word quite often. For example: 'cork' becomes 'cor'.

UNDERPLAYING THE CONSONANTS

Most European languages and English spoken in the West have a lot less emphasis applied on consonants, as opposed to the Indian languages. Therefore, someone who comes to India after having spent a considerable amount of time in the West tends to speak Indian languages by skimming over the consonants. He/she will need to relearn the pronunciation of consonants in the Indian context.

INTONATION

Intonation is the subtle changes in volume and cadence as we speak. We are not monotonous; in other words, the human speech does not sound robotic. There is a constant variation of loudness; certain words are emphasized more than others. We shall be talking about this in greater detail in our next chapter on voice modulation. In a nutshell, intonations are also related at a subliminal level to cultural influences and, therefore, vary in each language. This triggers the transference of intonation from one language to another spoken by the individual.

For example, when we speak the sentence, 'This coffee is really good', we tend to emphasize at least one word, 'this' or 'coffee' or 'really' as follows:

- *This* coffee is really good.
- This *coffee* is really good.
- This coffee is *really* good.

Now let us look at some examples:

- In the Tulu language, words are spoken very fast with the intonation at the very end. A Tulu-speaking person would, therefore, say, 'Thiscoffeeisverygood', followed by a big 'ah'.
- In Bengali, the entire sentence is stretched without too much emphasis on any of the words.
- In languages like Tamil, Malayalam or Kannada, each and every word is emphasized.

On balance, accent reduction or minimization is a process of learning new habits and patterns for speaking. As mentioned earlier, it is a difficult task because the cadences and inflections in our speech are deeply ingrained habits and although total elimination of these is not possible, the superimposed native accent can be mitigated to a great extent. However, as the task is not easy, one definitely needs to work with a speech therapist or diction teacher or accent coach to improve one's speaking skills.

The whole idea of learning about accents is to be able to achieve a neutral accent in whichever language you are performing – as a singer, as an actor, in your daily life as a corporate executive, as a newsreader, teacher, etc.

Having perfected your diction and accent, we move on to the next very important parameter – voice modulation.

9

VOICE MODULATION

A Matter of Flexibility or Emotion?

Modulation is a topic that is most sought after and talked about, whether it is by an actor, a singer, a CEO, or a news presenter. The most common phrases heard in a recording or dubbing studio are always 'modulate your voice' and 'your voice is flat'.

So, what is modulation? The dictionary definition of modulation is 'to change or to vary'. It means to have a variation in your voice. This can also be understood by looking at the opposite of modulation, which is a monotonous voice or 'one tone'. Modulation means varying your voice. Exactly what is it in the voice that we need to vary? There are numerous things that can be easily changed – the pitch, the volume and so on. We shall look into these a bit later.

Let us examine what the term 'modulation' means to different people:

- To an actor: it means to emote with the voice, allowing the sentiments of the role to seep into speech.
- To a singer: the melody, the harmony and the intense feelings underpinning the lyrics should all be reflected in the rendition, which calls for perfect modulation.
- To a news presenter or a CEO, voice modulation animates the talk, making it lively and interesting for the audience.
- To a teacher or a lawyer, modulation helps to put across their theories and deliver content effectively, with the right amount of emphasis and clarity.

In our day-to-day lives, we all use voice modulation. We express our feelings, our thoughts and concepts quite well. So, how does that happen? Are we all taught modulation as kids? No, it comes naturally to us because here the modulation is guided by our thought and the associated feeling. Therefore, if you are angry, the emotion raises your voice to express that anger. If you are expressing love, the sentiment infuses the right intonation into the voice to express that affection. Therefore, clarity of thoughts and ideas, and the will to convey these with precision provide intuitive guidance to take the right pauses and punctuations. This is what is known as an inside-out phenomenon.

However, if you are in a profession that requires you to use your voice, you may or may not actually feel the required emotions at the necessary juncture to auto-guide your voice. For example, an actor on set who is doing an angry scene may not be genuinely furious. In such cases, he needs to employ an outside-to-inside process wherein he deliberately decides and executes the loudness of his voice. Thus, one has to often pre-decide and employ techniques learnt in voice modulation to effectively convey emotions, feelings and concepts. This explains why the need to understand and learn various modulation techniques arises.

Learning the right techniques will make your vocal presentation interesting and captivating.

So, which are the aspects of your voice that can be manipulated at will? The parameters of voice which we discussed earlier – the pitch, the volume and the resonance – of course, can be tweaked, but certain other variations can also be included here as follows:

- Pitch or inflexion
- Loudness or dynamism
- Resonance or tone
- Speed or pace
- Punctuation or pause

Before we learn about each of these parameters, let me talk about a few important concepts. Firstly, your voice needs to be ready to perform the required variations. So, for at least two weeks, you will need to do all the flexibility exercises listed earlier in the chapter titled 'How to Get That Loud, Booming, Resonant Voice'. The flexibility of your voice is like the controls of your car, which respond to your will. If your car is in a bad shape, it will sputter, whine and refuse to obey your commands. Similarly, the concepts of variation may be there in your head, but the voice, which is your instrument, may not be responsive if it has not been exercised. Secondly, all variation across the five parameters will be guided by the content of what you wish to say. Therefore, whether you vary your pitch or volume, or modify the speed of your speech, etc., you will be guided by the content at all times. Although I had called it an outside-to-inside process, it eventually does turn out to be an inside-to-outside process because, with practice, the content gets internalized over time. Thirdly, a very important word of caution that I would want each one of you to keep in mind is that you should never over-modulate your voice.

OVER-MODULATION

If you vary too many parameters too often within a sentence, you will tend to sound overdramatic. So take a cue from your normal speech and activities, and ensure that the variations are minimal but effective. Over-modulation is also called 'hamming' in the world of acting. For example, if you emphasize every word in the sentence 'This coffee is really good', do you think you would sound good? Please try it out and see how it sounds. You need to stress only one word in a sentence with five or six words and maybe two words in longer sentences to bring it to life. This brings us to a very important concept, which I call 'key words'.

Key Words

The concept of key words is something that I find very useful. It is the backbone of voice modulation. Earlier, I have mentioned the various parameters that can be tweaked like pitch or volume. In order to use variations appropriately, the concept of key words is essential. The key word in any sentence is that special word which needs to be varied. For example, in the sentence 'This coffee is really good', the key word could be 'this', 'coffee', 'is', 'really' or even 'good'! The choice of the key word depends on various factors.

Every small sentence can have one key word and larger sentences, two or even three. As a general rule, adjectives form very good key words, as do proper nouns. Conjunctions like 'and', 'but' and 'so' also form good key words, especially in relation to pace. Therefore, stressing on these key words helps slow down your pace. Pronouns and verbs usually are not the first choices for key words unless the situation specially demands it.

The first factor, the content, is the most important. Therefore, if you want to praise the coffee you could use either 'coffee' or 'good'. If you want to convey just how good it is, you would place the emphasis on 'really' or 'good'. And if it's that particular cup of coffee that is impressive, you would stress on 'this' or 'is'.

The second factor is whether you are in the role of an actor, a singer, a voice-over artist or something else:

- For the actor the deciding factor on key words would be the emotions he wishes to portray, or the meaning he wishes to convey.

- As a singer, the key words depend on the mood of the song.
- For the newsreader, the key words are contingent on the information that is being telecast.
- For a teacher, the concepts to be conveyed in the lesson guides the choice of key words.

In the end, you will find that content always guides your selection of key words.

Once the key word is selected, based on your preference and vocal capabilities, you can vary pitch, loudness, resonance, pace or punctuation for emphasis. These may often be interconnected and you could use more than one of them. Apart from selecting a key word and doing a variation on that, these parameters can also be varied in general over the entire sentence, paragraph, page or the full length of the content. These concepts are elaborated in the following sections.

Let us examine these parameters individually and see how we can vary them to bring about voice modulation:

PITCH OR INFLECTION

As we have understood from the earlier chapters, pitch is the frequency of your voice or the rate at which your vocal cords vibrate. As the number of vibrations per second increases, your voice's pitch rises, sounding shriller, and conversely, as the vibration rate dips, the pitch becomes lower or deeper (also called 'bass'). We also know that the rate of vibration depends on the length and thickness of your vocal cords, and the tightening and relaxation of the muscles around them. Therefore, by using the exercises mentioned earlier to stretch the flexibility of your voice, you can effectively increase the range of your voice. I understand that a new term 'range' has come up here. The range of your voice is the entire spectrum from the lowest to the highest possible pitch that your voice can hit. The human voice has a range of one-and-a-half to two octaves (eight notes in an octave). However, while speaking, we do not use more than one octave. The extended range is used only in singing. Everyone can recognize a low pitch, a medium pitch and a high pitch. For example, Amitabh Bachchan has a low-pitched voice while Lata Mangeshkar, a high-pitched voice.

How do you vary your pitch to effectively modulate your voice? There are two ways of doing this. One is to vary the pitch of a specific word, or set of words, to create an effect, as discussed in the key words section. The key words could be either at a lower or higher pitch compared to the rest of the sentence. For example, let us take the same sentence used earlier when we discussed key words 'This coffee is really good'. If my key word is 'really', I could either drop the pitch at the word, or raise it. Pitch variations are not as commonly used as loudness variations. Most people would use a loudness variation for the word 'really', which is a lot easier than pitch variations. Pitch variations require a lot of practice and well-honed voice control. However, once achieved, they are far more effective.

Second, deliberately changing the pitch of the entire sentence, staying within your natural vocal range, creates a different mood, ambience, drama and emotion to whatever you are saying. For example, if I say the following sentence in a very low-pitched voice, 'Why are you so late?', it communicates a sense of hopelessness and helplessness. However, if it is said in a high pitch, it denotes anger or frustration. So happiness or excitement will take on a higher pitch, whereas sorrow or solemnity will take on a lower pitch. For actors and voice-over artists, the change in pitch would also depend on the character that they are playing. Older characters will have lower pitch while younger characters would have higher pitch. For example, in the movie, *Haseena Maan Jayegi*, actor Govinda used a lower pitch while playing the character of an elderly uncle. Pitch variations can be based on the characteristics of the person they are portraying. An example would be in the movie, *Agneepath*, where Amitabh Bachchan used a very low pitch to play the character, Vijay, who was driven by rage and revenge.

For singers, pitch is a very important parameter because singing involves using the voice in the entire possible range. Therefore, choosing the right pitch is a key factor. We shall talk about this in greater detail in the chapter titled 'The Singer's Voice'. To a great extent, the mood of the song determines the pitch at which the song is set.

Many a time, changing the pitch could also be a way of indicating parentheses. A teacher or a lawyer could probably lower or increase their pitch to drive home a point. A newsreader could be using a higher pitch to dramatize an event. As mentioned earlier, pitch variations will need a lot more practice compared to the input required to develop the loudness variation.

LOUDNESS OR DYNAMISM

Loudness is fairly straightforward to understand. It is the volume. I wish changing the voice's volume was as easy as pressing a button on the TV remote but, unfortunately, it isn't! This brings us again to our skill and control over the pliancy of our voice. I cannot stress enough on the importance of working on the general flexibility levels of your voice.

One level of loudness variation is used in your key words. Loudness is directly related to the amount of air that you expel. If you want to be loud, you need to throw out lots of air very quickly; the same amount of air can be used for a longer duration if your volume is low. Voice projection is all about how much air you throw out.

As with pitch, loudness can be used in two ways. Firstly, the key words can be louder or softer in comparison to the rest of the sentence, thus producing a variation. So, take the same old sentence for example, 'This coffee is really good!' If you have chosen 'really' as the key word, you can say it louder or softer than the rest of the sentence, thus causing a variation. Secondly, the volume of the entire conversation or dialogue or song can be loud or soft depending on the emotions, thoughts, characters and situations. Therefore, if you're angry, your overall loudness will be more; if you are sad, less. A sports news presenter can be very loud if the issue is dynamic; not at all if it is one of national sorrow. So, thoughts and emotions like excitement, enthusiasm, sarcasm, pity, wonder, cynicism and sadness can be expressed by pitch or loudness variations.

For singers, certain songs are set at a particular high-energy loudness level and some derive their melody by being really soft. A teacher with a class full of toddlers probably uses high loudness levels and a CEO trying to clinch his deal is going to speak softly. I cannot stress enough on the importance of variation and mastery of voice modulation.

RESONANCE OR TONE

Resonance is like an echo and it depends on which part of the vocal passage vibrates the maximum with air. As mentioned in the earlier chapters, if it vibrates more in the throat region, it is a low resonance. If the vibration is in the mouth, middle resonance. And if nasal, high resonance. As we speak, certain sounds are naturally of low resonance, like 'ha'; some have middle resonance, like 'ka', 'ga', 'ta', 'da, 'va' and so on. The sounds of high or nasal resonance are 'ma' and 'na'. Therefore, our normal speaking voice is a mixture of all resonances. Nevertheless, for modulation purposes, resonance can also be a method of voice variation.

As with pitch and loudness, the key words could be spoken with a different resonance when compared to the rest of the sentence. Again, using 'really' as the key word in our standard example 'This coffee is really good', it can be said with a lower or higher resonance in comparison to the rest of the sentence. However, this form of variation is quite rare.

The use of variation in resonance or tone is popular mainly in the acting line for characterization. Supposing you are playing role of an elderly character, use of lower resonances alongside lower pitches can create a very authentic voice. Higher resonances can be used if playing a younger character. For example, Amitabh Bachchan in the movie, *Aakhree Raasta*, used a lower resonance and pitch while playing the father who was an elderly person. Similarly, Hrithik Roshan used higher resonances while playing the character of a boy with a low mental age in the movie, *Koi Mil Gaya*. Therefore, resonance along with pitch is an excellent tool for actors portraying other age groups.

Resonance also plays a key role for singers. There are many singers who predominantly use nasal resonance and this is their signature style. For example, the legendary Mukesh and more recently, Himesh Reshammiya, use nasal resonance to set their style.

SPEED OR PACE

Pace refers to the speed, rhythm, timing and tempo of your speech. There could be various possibilities of variation here. The most important factor to be considered with this form of variation is diction. If your style of speaking is one of high speed, clarity of diction or pronunciation needs to be maintained. The common pitfalls of fast speech would be swallowing word endings and mispronunciation of cluster consonants like 'st', 'sk' and so on. On the other hand, a very slow-paced drawl would require payment of close attention to certain aspects of accents like lengthening of vowels and syllabic breaks.

Any television commercial or newsfeed, if it had no pausing, would have zero impact on the audience, even if the content of the commercial or news broadcast is fascinating. If it is too fast, it is almost like a rapid-fire instruction given to you. However, if it is too slow, as 'The ... double murder ... is ... shaking up ... all ... middle-class ... families ... and their ... values', the audience will rapidly lose interest. A slow pace is downright boring, to say the least. Therefore, whether it is a newsfeed or a commercial, a presentation by a CEO or a teacher expounding concepts and theories, alternating the speech tempo is crucial. This places importance on certain words, phrases and ideas and gives an edge to your presentation.

The key words and phrases (discussed at the beginning of this chapter) will be the highlighted areas at which to slow down or accelerate. Therefore, you can slow down on key words and pick up pace over the not-so-important aspects of a presentation. Hence, in the following sentence, 'This mountainous region grows numerous fruits like apples, pears, apricots, peaches, plums, raspberries and blueberries', the key words could be 'mountainous region' and 'numerous fruits'. So you could read the sentence as, 'This ... mountainous ... region (include loudness, pitch or resonance elevation) grows ... numerous ... fruits (again, include loudness, pitch or resonance elevation)', and then, use a faster pace as you list all the fruits.

As with loudness, pitch and resonance, certain forms of content can, overall, be faster or slower. This is not as important or as difficult as the pacing within sentences and paragraphs.

PUNCTUATION OR PAUSE

Punctuation, for me, ties in with all the four variations mentioned above, along with the concept of key words. Selection of key words and whether to vary them with loudness or pitch or resonance, where to take the pauses and which words to emphasize, is all about punctuation. Although punctuation literally means pauses, I would like to deal with punctuation as a more rounded concept where you think about it not just as a pause but also as key words to enhance with the help of variations of loudness, pitch and resonance. In a nutshell, punctuation is emphasis by pausing. These pauses will be guided by key words; the extent of emphasis and lengths of pauses are expressed using pitch, loudness and resonance. Furthermore, punctuation is closely related to pacing as well, especially in the sense of the overall substance of the paragraph, presentation or concept.

Punctuation by itself could have various effects on what you are trying to say. Firstly, it can change the meaning completely. For example, in the following sentence, 'When did I say Rekha stole Radha's purse?' it could mean different things depending on the punctuation:

- '*When*, did I say Rekha stole Radha's purse?' would imply I am asking the person the time I said it – today, yesterday, last week and so on (the key word is 'when' and one can stress on it using any form of voice variation at one's disposal).

- When did *I*, say Rekha stole Radha's purse? This means the information may be right, but I did not say it (the key word to be stressed is 'I').
- When did I say *Rekha*, stole Radha's purse? This means I told you the information but it is not Rekha who stole the purse but somebody else (the key word to be stressed here is 'Rekha').
- When did I say Rekha stole *Radha's*, purse? This means I told you Rekha stole somebody's purse, but not Radha's (the key word to be stressed here is 'Radha's').

Alternatively, punctuation may not necessarily change the meaning, but can increase or decrease the impact of what you are saying. In the sentence 'This coffee is really good', if I stress on 'really' and say it as 'this coffee is *really*, good', it shows that the coffee was really good and I mean it. Whereas if I stress on 'coffee', saying 'this *coffee*, is really good', it would indicate that I am comparing this coffee to something else.

In conclusion, modulation with all its elements can make the difference between a great performance and a good performance for an actor, interesting versus uninteresting news presentation, or a deal clinched versus a deal fallen through for a corporate executive. In the subsequent chapters, we will deal with the implications of voice modulation for various professional voice users.

One exercise that will go a long way in increasing the flexibility of your voice and, in turn, your voice modulation, is learning to sing. This is elaborated in the next chapter.

10

WHY SHOULD YOU LEARN TO SING?

Singing Your Way to Speech

Often actors and other professional voice users have been advised to take singing lessons to improve the suppleness of their voice. In fact, many acting schools in India include music lessons in their curriculum. However, this is actually a double-edged sword and can cut both ways. Although there are many advantages in learning music, which I shall talk about shortly, I'd like to put in a word of caution here. Singing is like an athletic activity for the voice, as compared to speaking, which is like walking. Therefore, if you have not learnt to use the voice from the belly and are still using it from the throat (we have talked about this in the chapter on breathing and I am sure you have understood and learnt this skill by now), even a few singing lessons can damage your voice. Also, musical aptitude is an inborn talent and if you don't have this talent, you will struggle to sing and, in the process, hurt your voice. So I would rather advise you to focus on all the exercises meant for actors which will also help you achieve the same skills.

However, if you have an aptitude for singing, please go ahead and learn, because there are great advantages in learning to sing for an actor.

Let us examine some basics of singing. We all know that the basics of singing are the seven notes, namely Sa, Re, Ga, Ma, Pa, Dha, Ni in Indian music. What exactly happens when you sing the seven notes? The pitch of your voice ascends from very low to very high and then descends from very high to very low. It is not an arbitrary, but rather a graded, ascent and descent of the pitch of your voice. The pitch difference between these sequential notes remains constant. The following line diagram (Figure 10.1) illustrates this point:

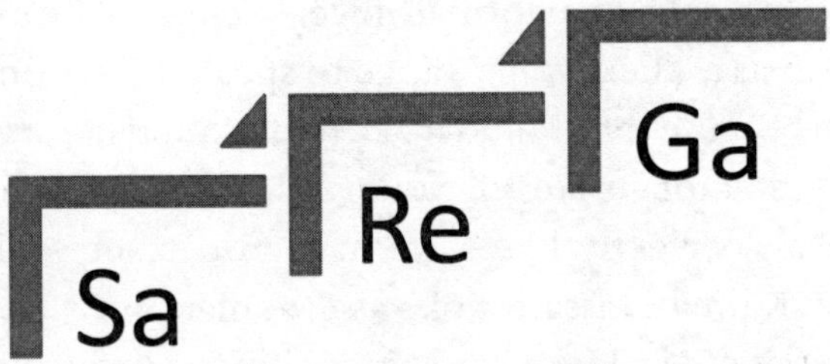

FIGURE 10.1: Steps of Sa Re Ga...

As you can see, the height of the step, or the ascent, is the same for each step. For example, if Sa has a pitch of 220 hertz, Re is 230, Ga is 240, Ma is 250, and so on. The entire range of eight notes, from the initial Sa to the last Sa, is called one octave. A normal human voice has a range of two to three octaves at the most. Therefore, it is no mean task to sing Sa, Re, Ga, Ma, Pa, Dha, Ni, although for someone with musical aptitude it would seem like a breeze. You can understand this concept better if you listen to a non-singer struggling to sing the scale of Sa, Re, Ga, Ma. Therefore, if you can carry a tune, you can achieve great flexibility and control over your voice, especially in pitch variations. If you train for advanced musical skills, you can increase your range up to four or five octaves by going into the head voice or the falsetto.

What is falsetto (false voice) or head voice? In simple terms, it is using a very high-pitched voice which is beyond your normal range. We have already discussed the vocal range which all of us have – two to three octaves – and falsetto is something that goes beyond that. Technically, the vocal cords vibrate quite differently for falsetto compared to the vibrations of a normal voice. We normally use what is known as a 'chest voice' range to speak. Men don't use a falsetto because that would make them sound like a woman. But as an actor or singer, you can learn it, and then you can speak perfectly like a woman. For example, look at the way Kamal Hassan spoke as a woman in *Chachi 420*, or John Travolta in *Hairspray*. Many women singers use their falsettos to sing, and do it wonderfully.

I would like to put in a word of caution here. Don't try and use the falsetto on your own. It is an extremely specialized skill. Please learn it only from a music teacher.

What also needs to be taken into consideration is that

the other two parameters of voice, namely loudness and resonance, are also related to the pitch. In other words, changes in one of the parameters will automatically reflect in the other two parameters. Loudness is at its maximum in the mid-range of your pitch, and tapers down as it approaches the lowest or the highest end of the pitch range. Figure 5.1 in chapter five explains this relationship between loudness and pitch in the bell curve diagram. For the sake of convenience and comparison (see later) it is being reproduced as Figure 10.2.

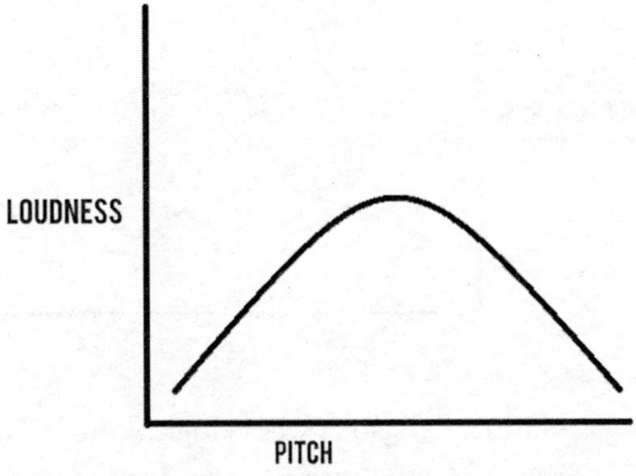

FIGURE 10.2: Bell curve diagram showing the relationship between loudness and pitch in normal speech

Although this happens to us during normal speech, it does not seem very obvious. Have you noticed that when you try to speak at a higher or lower pitch, you are not as loud as your natural pitch? However, we don't encounter this problem in normal day-to-day speech because we generally speak in our natural pitch, by default. On the other hand, when you sing, you need to use lower and higher pitches as per the demands of the song. That is when you realize that the volume is not consistent. In any case, with practice, the loudness at the lower and higher ends of the pitch range can be increased with proper use of breathing and other techniques. It can be made to look like Figure 10.3, where the bell curve flattens when higher and lower pitches are raised, as in singing.

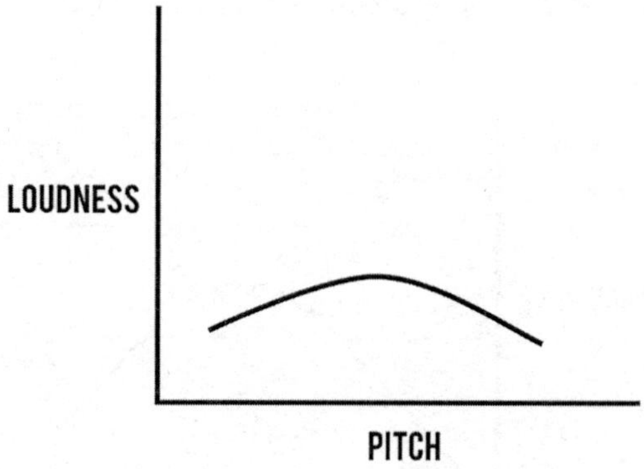

FIGURE 10.3: Another bell curve where higher and lower pitches are raised compared to normal speech

As a professional voice user, you may need to vary the pitch of your voice frequently and simultaneously sustain the high volume. This is where your music training pays off. For example, if you are voicing for an elderly person as a voice-over professional, you may be required to speak in a much lower pitch than your natural pitch. Consequently, the volume will substantially reduce. However, if you have been trained to sing, you would have better volume even at the lower pitches. For example, Amitabh Bachchan as the old man in *Aakhree Raasta*, Shah Rukh Khan as the old prisoner in *Veer-Zaara*, Govinda as the uncle in *Haseena Maan Jaayegi* or Rekha as the grandmother in *Krrish* displayed their amazing voice skills. A man playing the role of a woman or a child would need to use a very high-pitched voice. Examples for this would be Kamal Hassan in *Chachi 420* and Hrithik Roshan as a retarded young boy in *Koi Mil Gaya*. Hrithik also used his resonance which we shall discuss later. Your singing lessons will help maintain good volume despite the altered pitch.

Pitch is associated with age. As children, both boys and girls have high-pitched, shrill voices. Girls continue to retain their high pitch to an extent as they grow up, but the male voice undergoes drastic changes with the onset of puberty. It grows deep and gruff. As both men and women age beyond sixty or seventy, the pitch drops further by half an octave. Therefore, you will require to modify your pitch to suit the age of the character you portray. Furthermore, the changed pitch needs to be perfectly audible as well. Again, this is where musical training helps tremendously.

The other parameter that is so closely related to loudness and pitch is resonance. These three are actually inseparable. Any change in one will affect the other two. The lower pitches will automatically keep the resonances lower and the result will sound throaty. When you deliberately lower your pitch, the volume automatically diminishes and even the quality of resonance will drop. Therefore, you need to make a conscious effort to maintain the resonance at the mouth level while using a lower pitch. On the other hand, for higher pitches, the resonance will spontaneously shift to nasal mode, which again needs to be checked or corrected. For example, when Hrithik Roshan used a high-pitched voice in *Koi Mil Gaya*, he sounded extremely nasal, but in this case it suited the role very well.

IT'S ABOUT FLEXIBILITY

As a professional voice user, what you need the most is flexibility. You need the ability to use your voice in different pitches, intensities and resonances. As an actor, you will need to speak like different people or characters. As a corporate executive, the various parameters of your voice can be used to bring alive your presentations and talks. As a teacher, you probably need to rely on your voice amplification skills more than the other parameters. And as a newsreader, you will have to use your voice flexibility skills to hold viewer interest.

Learning to sing is hard work. However, it is the best way to achieve voice flexibility. No other method can give you that kind of flexibility. But it is not the only method. The idea is to choose the mode that suits you best, and not to blindly plunge into music lessons. I shall not give any exercise on singing here, but rather advise you to find a good music teacher.

APPLICATIONS

Singing in tune requires a lot more breath support and control than speech. Therefore, if you can sing well, you probably have much more lung capacity than someone who never sings. This in turn will give you many advantages like:

- Strong and powerful voice
- Ability to project your voice
- Flexibility of voice
- Endurance of voice
- Better capacity to emote
- Better control of voice
- Easy to modulate your voice
- Protection from voice damage
- Better tone of voice

Now that you have mastered all aspects of voice and speech and have learnt to use them effectively in your chosen field of work, the only thing left is to develop the ability to carry on vocalizing for long stretches at a time. This is addressed in chapter twelve, on vocal endurance.

11

WHAT CAN GO WRONG WITH YOUR VOICE?

Prevention Is Better Than Cure

In this book, my aim has been to provide useful information, tips, guidance and exercises to all professional voice users; and if I do not inform you about some of the things that could possibly go wrong with your voice and the preventive measures that can be taken, my endeavour would be incomplete.

DEFINITION OF VOICE DISORDER

Voice disorder is a medical condition involving abnormal pitch, loudness or quality of sound produced by the vocal cords, which in turn affects your voicing and speech production. I would personally divide voice disorders into two categories:

- Those disorders which are not related to how and how much you use your voice, and are purely medical conditions that could affect anyone irrespective of their manner of voicing.
- Those disorders which are directly related to how and how much you use your voice. This category section is probably more pertinent to professional voice users.

VOICE DISORDERS DUE TO EXTERNAL CAUSES

I would like to list a few conditions that can cause voice problems. These conditions are because of some external cause and will need the medical input of an ENT specialist and/or a speech pathologist.

Puberphonia

Puberphonia is a condition where an adult male sounds like a woman. All boys have a girlish voice before puberty. At puberty, it changes into a low-pitched voice. In some cases, this transition does not happen due to various reasons.

Vocal Cord Paralysis

One or both the vocal cords can get paralysed due to various medical and neurological conditions. This results in hoarseness or loss of voice.

Cancer of Vocal Cords

Like any part of the body, cancer could strike the vocal

cords; naturally, medical care would be necessary to save the voice.

Vocal Atrophy

With age, the vocal cords can lose their strength and elasticity. This condition is called atrophy of the vocal cords. This results in a weak and hoarse voice.

Injury or Trauma

Any severe injury to the throat region can damage the vocal cords.

Bowing of Vocal Cords

Bending of the vocal cords due to age and various medical conditions result in hoarseness.

Vocal Cord Infections

An upper respiratory infection can progress downwards to involve the larynx and result in inflammation of the vocal cords, causing pain, laryngeal cough and rasping voice with fever. These symptoms need to be treated by a doctor.

Vocal Polyps and Cysts

Benign growths sometimes occur on the vocal cords, resulting in hoarseness of voice, often needing medical or surgical treatment.

VOICE DISORDERS DUE TO OVERUSE OR MISUSE OF VOICE

Having mentioned some of the medical conditions that affect the voice, I'd now like to elaborate on those conditions which arise purely due to overuse and misuse of voice. As a professional voice user, you are repeatedly required to use your voice a lot and also in different ways. Although you conscientiously practise all the methods that I recommend and have excellent endurance and fitness regimens, there could be times when something goes wrong with your voice. Naturally, you will need to visit a doctor or speech therapist. However, it pays to stay alert and recognize these signs early, so that there is no long-lasting or permanent damage. Here is a list of warning signs which should set alarm bells ringing and induce you to make a beeline to the doctor:

- Harsh, gravelly, or rough voice
- Pain or difficulty when swallowing
- Feeling like there's a lump stuck in your throat
- Dry mouth
- Clearing your throat more than two times an hour
- Frequent hoarseness
- Voice loss
- Pitch breaking or voice cracking
- Vocal fatigue especially at night
- Voice power gradually diminishing after talking for an extended period of time

Let me also educate you a bit on the three likely medical

conditions that could result as an outcome of overuse and misuse of one's voice:

Acute Laryngitis

In simple terms, a swelling in the vocal cords makes the voice sound hoarse. There could be slight pain while talking, and also symptoms of cough, reduced volume and inability to use the voice in its entire range. In Hindi this syndrome is described as '*awaaz baithi hui hai*'). It is known in English as 'inability to produce a voice' or a 'complete voice shutdown'. This usually resolves in a couple of days after a period of voice rest, and requires no medication.

Chronic Laryngitis

This again is an inflammation or swelling of the vocal cords on a long-term basis. If you don't take care of your acute laryngitis and continue to misuse your voice, it could lead to chronic laryngitis. This requires voice rest for a longer period; and after the throat recovers, it is wise to train the voice again in order to prevent recurrence.

Vocal Nodules

Chronic laryngitis, if neglected for over six months to a year, could lead to the growth of small benign nodules on your vocal cords. These are very common in singers, especially if they persist in singing in the wrong pitch and failing to use proper breath support. Therefore, this syndrome is also known as 'singer's nodules'. It will require medical and surgical treatment, as well as speech therapy.

In conclusion, I suggest you read all the previous chapters with attention to detail and cherish, train and develop your voice so that you never have any problems. I present a quick guide on the best way to care for your voice in the next chapter.

12

VOCAL ENDURANCE

The Ability to Go on and on...

Vocal endurance is the ability to sing or talk for long periods of time without the voice losing its power or quality, or growing fatigued. It means having the same strength and quality of voice at the end of the performance as at the beginning. As an actor, sometimes the shoots and dubbing go on for over eight hours at a stretch. The same is true for singers, with seven-day weeks of interminable rehearsals for months on end. And in those long hours, one is expected to use one's voice in various pitches at varying degrees of loudness. This puts a tremendous strain on the voice. It's a catch-22 situation. The rehearsal itself, which is essential for a polished performance, tires your voice. The position of the teacher, the lawyer and the CEO is the same, although their use of the voice is not as glamourized as that of actors and singers. Unless properly prepared, this kind of prolonged use of one's vocal abilities could permanently damage the vocal cords. Therefore, even for a person with excellent voice skills in terms of modulation, diction and accent, and excellent acting and singing talent, lack of endurance and strength to carry on vocalizing for long stretches of time will render their talents useless.

This kind of endurance is comparable to the stamina of an athlete. Just as an athlete increases his muscular strength to perform for long periods of time without fatigue, the voice user also needs to improve the musculature of the entire vocal apparatus and its stamina. In this sense, we can call them vocal athletes. They need to work on not just the techniques, but also strength and stamina. Having said all this, there is a difference between an athlete and a voice user. The anatomy of the voice-producing apparatus, as discussed earlier, is fragile compared to the muscle sets worked out by an athlete. The constantly vibrating vocal cords are so delicate that it is an uphill task to improve the complex structure without risking a rupture. If overused, the various muscle structures inside the throat swell up, resulting in hoarseness or even pain while speaking. Unlike other muscles' soreness, treatment by medication is not very effective here. The only antidote to voice fatigue is rest (absolute silence) which could be difficult when the line of work requires you to be speaking all day long.

Therefore, the importance of resting the voice, vocal hygiene and an appropriate vocal fitness regimen cannot be overrated. These voice workouts should be preceded by warm up exercises and alternated with periods of rest. The warm-up is like oiling the machinery of the vocal muscles and helps to increase endurance and strength. To sum up, endurance will need:

- Proper breathing techniques with the know-how to harness it
- Daily vocal fitness regimen
- Vocal hygiene
- Warm-up routines

Let us consider all these factors:

PROPER BREATHING TECHNIQUES

For this, please refer to chapter three, on breathing.

DAILY VOCAL FITNESS REGIMEN

Just like the athlete, one needs to develop a regimen to exercise each and every muscle involved in voicing; which in turn means exercising the generator, vibrator, resonator and articulator. Here are some basic exercises:

HEALTHY VOCAL HYGIENE

Don'ts

- Smoke tobacco or any other substance.
- Drink alcohol or coffee or dairy products on the day before a performance.

- Become a cheerleader or shout and scream at sporting events.
- Go to loud clubs or bars.
- Talk on a bus, train or airplane or try to be heard in noisy places like bars, large family gatherings, sport events, etc.
- Vocalize a sneeze.
- Phonate while yawning.
- Stay up late the night before a performance.
- Sing outdoors or without a mike.
- Cough or clear your throat incessantly.
- Try to talk while you have a cold or sore throat.
- Sing at a pitch which is higher or lower than your optimum one or try to change your natural speaking tone.
- Sing if it hurts to swallow.
- Over-sing (if you are hoarse after singing, it means you are over-singing).
- Whisper.
- Scream.
- Cry.
- Talk too much.
- Talk a lot on the day of your performance.
- Overeat before a concert/recording. Your stomach should be only half full.
- Get stressed out.
- Visit places with foul, polluted air or inhale cooking fumes, smoke from puja havans, etc. Everything you breathe passes through your vocal instrument.

Dos

- Speak at your natural pitch.
- Support your speaking voice just as when singing.
- Get plenty of rest.
- Be happy.
- Eat sensibly.
- Cherish your vocal cords.
- Avoid dry climates.
- Drink lots of water (at least eight glasses a day).

WARM-UP ROUTINES

Having a good warm-up regimen for the voice is a sensible way to get the vocal apparatus ready for performance. Similar to oiling a piece of machinery, it prepares the vocal apparatus and prevents any injury that might result from suddenly bursting into song or speech thereby straining it. Here is a quick guide to warm-up exercises. There is a detailed version of it in the chapter titled 'The Complete Vocal Exercise Guide'.

Quick warm-up exercises

- Stand in perfect alignment (erect, with the spine straight); do neck–head range-of-motion exercises. Head turn: look to the right over your shoulder, palm against cheek to increase the stretch. Now go to the left. Head tilt: bring ear to shoulder, the hand across the top of the head for extra stretching. Now nod in this position. Do this on both sides. Bend head forward, gazing down, then move your gaze upward as you move your head up. Keep your jaw relaxed throughout.

- Shoulder shrugs: raise shoulders up, breathing in through the nose, and drop them, breathing out through the mouth. Roll shoulders backwards. Do arm circles.
- Bend over, dangle the arms down. Trill the lips while in this position. Roll up into standing position.
- Massage the jaw muscles and jiggle them. (Picture a big dog with loose lips and floppy tongue!)
- Lip stretches: pout your lips and then retract them. Purse your lips and then flatten and stretch them.
- Tongue stretches: 'Count' your teeth with your tongue, inside and outside the bridges. 'Tenderize' your tongue with your teeth. Stick out your tongue; now count from one to four. (Yes, this sounds funny.)
- Practise tongue tip sounds without moving your jaw: la lee lay lee. Ta tee tay tee. Na nee nay nee. Lucky lady lucky laddie.
- Breathe in and out slowly, focusing on abdominal breathing. Breathe in, belly moves out. Breathe out, belly moves in.
- Yawn and sigh on the vowel sounds: ah, ee, oo.
- Recite 'Mary had a little lamb' with your tongue sticking out. Do this before you go out in public!

VOICE REST

As mentioned earlier in this chapter, voice rest is a very important part of the healthy vocal fitness and hygiene regimen. Periods of voice rest are very effective in maintaining a great voice. It is very simple to understand the concept of voice rest if we relate it to a dietary plan. If you give yourself a holiday from your weight-loss programme that allows you to have an intake of a fixed number of calories and gets you to exercise for a certain amount of time every day, you will need to compensate by doing a little more after the break. In other words, you will probably have to eat less and exercise more during the subsequent days.If you have walked a lot, say for ten hours in a day, or if an athlete has played a very gruelling match lasting many hours, it makes sense to rest for a day or two before doing it again so that the body gets time to recuperate and re-energize. Similarly, if you have overused or misused your voice (described in detail in the chapter titled 'What Can Go Wrong with Your Voice?'), you need to compensate by giving your voice complete rest.

So, what is voice rest? Speaking less? No, not making any sound at all is voice rest. It means to use only non-verbal modes of communication like email, text messages on a cellphone and chat rooms, or get back to basics and use a pen and notepaper. Complete voice rest means no voice for the stipulated period of time. Do you think it's easy? Not really. Firstly, if you are using your voice in your profession as an actor or singer, taking complete voice rest for one day would mean rearranging a lot of your work schedule. Secondly, if you are a talkative kind of person, voice rest for an entire day would be sheer torture.

Therefore, if you are taking a well-deserved voice rest to compensate for all the overuse, schedule it in a planned way into your non-working hours; this can be done for half a day or a few hours. However, if the voice rest has been therapeutically prescribed for some disorder that you have developed in your voice, you may have to go mute for perhaps even up to a week. My word of advice would be for you to incorporate regular, short periods of voice rest and religiously follow vocal fitness and hygiene regimens to ensure that your voice stays robust.

13

DOS AND DON'TS

An A-to-Z Guide to the Dos and Don'ts

A

Acidity

Acidity, acid reflux or regurgitation is a major cause of hoarseness. Whenever the acid levels in the stomach are too high or when we lie down, there is a possibility of the acid rising up the food pipe and reaching the throat. Although the stomach's lining can handle these digestive acids, the throat's membranes cannot. The acid irritates and inflames the mucosa of the throat, including the voice box, and causes redness, swelling and a raspy voice. This could worsen unless the underlying cause, the acidity, is treated. The problem could be quite serious and can even result in development of vocal nodules leading to severe vocal damage. The measures you need to take to preserve your voice are:

- Drink lots of water
- Cut down on spicy and oily food
- Relax and reduce stress in your life
- Consult with a doctor as soon as possible

Alcohol

Alcohol consumption is associated with dehydration in the body – loss of water. As a result, when alcohol has been consumed, the sensitive membranes of the mouth, throat and voice box become dry. The vocal cords are very delicate and need to be frequently lubricated with water. If you use your voice a lot after a few alcoholic drinks, the lack of lubrication is likely to damage the fragile vocal tissues.

Furthermore, alcohol consumption lowers inhibitions resulting in loss of self-restraint causing one to grow raucous and garrulous after a few drinks. This, coupled with the dehydration of the larynx can do dreadful damage to one's precious voice. Therefore, a dedicated voice user who values his voice, should avoid alcohol as much as possible, if not altogether.

Alcohol should be strictly avoided for at least twenty-four hours prior to a performance, so that the vocal cords remain in perfect shape for the final show.

Attitude

For a good voice, it is necessary to have a good attitude – both mental and physical. Your voice reflects your attitude. Be strong, bold, cheerful and confident!

Airway

Since the voice ultimately emerges from our airways, any congestion or infection of the airways will affect the voice. Prompt treatment is needed for all airway problems.

Aspiration

Many a time, when we eat or drink in a hurry, we end up aspirating the food or drink, trapping the food particles in the air passages. This leads to a hacking cough in order to expel the crumbs. Be careful while eating and drinking, because violent coughing can injure the voice apparatus.

Abuse

One of the prime reasons for voice related problems is vocal abuse. We tend to scream, strain, stretch and shout, without thinking of the havoc wreaked upon the larynx. This kind of abuse to one's voice should be avoided at all costs. If you are an actor, you need to refrain from yelling yourself hoarse at get-togethers, picnics and parties, avoid throwing temper tantrums and hollering at people and not go carousing, carolling and chorus singing or singing bhajans, etc. All these activities, although very enjoyable, will strain the voice.

Acceptance and Acknowledgement

For a professional voice user, accepting, acknowledging and cherishing their precious voice is of paramount importance.

Don't take your voice for granted; treasure it, or it will let you down when you need it most.

Awareness

Every actor needs to be extremely aware about the state of his voice and about the environment. Stay alert and be careful about when, where, what and how you speak.

B

Breathing

We have discussed in the chapter on breathing about how breathing is the lifeline to our voice. Learn deep breathing techniques and stick with them. This is probably one of the most important aspects of voice production and voice enhancement. Don't forget – breathe deeply.

C

Cough

Every time we cough, we put a strain on the vocal cords. If you have had a cough for a prolonged period of time, you need to get it diagnosed and treated at the earliest. Not only does the cough interfere with your speech, it also increases friction within the vocal cords and can lead to damage.

Cigarettes

For a good voice, cigarette smoking is a big no-no. The smoke irritates the voice box (and the lungs) and can cause chronic irritation. In the long run, as we all know, it can cause permanent damage to the voice box and the lungs – even cause cancer of these parts – which will be the end of a good voice.

Coffee

While coffee makes us feel good, its caffeine content tends to dehydrate our bodies, including vocal cords. Avoid coffee, if not every day, at least twenty-four hours before a performance.

Compensation

If you have screamed, shouted and abused your voice on one day, you have to take a 'voice off' day on the morrow to compensate for the strain. Otherwise, the condition of your voice will deteriorate and you will need medical treatment to heal.

Cold Beverages

Drinking cold drinks, cold water, etc., does not directly harm the voice, as the beverages enter the food passage without touching the vocal cords. However, with a basic knowledge of physics, we are aware that heat causes expansion and cold causes contraction. Therefore, if you drink something cold during a dubbing session, it will tend to contract the throat muscles, making voice production difficult. A hot drink, on the other hand, will relax the throat and help speech.

D

Dehydration

Any cause of dehydration – drinking inadequate amounts of fluids, too much heat and humidity in the environment, alcohol, coffee, air travel and medications – can ruin the voice. Drink lots of water and other fluids, all day long, to keep up your hydration.

Drugs

Many of the medicines that we take commonly, have a tendency to dehydrate the body or cause water retention. Both these extremes are bad for the voice. Keep medicine usage to minimum, and if you are on medications that either increase or decrease the water content in your tissues, take care not to abuse your voice.

E

Effort and Ease

Voicing should always be effortless and with ease. If you are struggling to speak or sing, it means you are using the wrong pitch, wrong technique, poor breath support; or you are in a noisy environment. The moment you feel a strain, stop speaking. Something is wrong, and until you rectify that don't ruin your voice by forcing out speech.

Elasticity

The voice and vocal cords should be elastic for the best range and voice modulation. Don't forget to do your exercises to maintain your voice's suppleness.

F

Fumes

Fumes of any sort – chemical vapours, smoke from burning wood, poojas or havans, cigarettes or incense sticks – irritate the voice, and therefore, need to be avoided as much as possible.

Fear

Stage fright, comprised of fear and anxiety, often exists before and during a performance on stage or delivering one's dialogue. The tension constricts the chest and throat impeding optimum voice production. One needs to be free from stress or worry and be relaxed to produce a good voice.

Food

There are a lot of myths about spicy or oily food causing voice problems. In reality, these don't have any direct impact on the voice because they don't come anywhere near the vocal cords. However, if you have a performance, you need to use your belly to produce a good voice, and it is always good not to overeat. Spicy and oily food can produce heartburn and regurgitation, which indirectly affect the voice. If you are prone to these conditions, it is better to avoid spicy food.

G

Gum

Many actors are in the habit of chewing gum. This tends to overuse the jaw muscles, causing soreness and tension in them. Therefore, in order to maintain a pristine voice condition, it is better to avoid chewing gum.

H

Honey

Honey and warm water, or even plain honey is good for the voice. Honey soothes the upper throat. It does not directly touch the voice box. After it is digested in the stomach, the natural goodness of honey permeates the body with its built-in healing properties that help to clear phlegm and strengthen the voice.

Hoarse Voice

Hoarseness, for whatever reason, is a warning signal to be heeded instantly. One must immediately stop using their voice and let if rest. Due to tight schedules, most actors continue to dub even if their voice is raspy. This not only diminishes the quality of voice output, it also tends to damage and inflame the voice box further.

I

Irritation

Any sort of throat irritation will weaken the voice. The moment the throat or larynx feels sore, you should remove yourself from that environment, in the interests of preserving your voice.

Imitation

All of us like to imitate our favourite actors or singers. However, remember that your voice is unique. Mimicry inflicts tremendous pressure on the vocal apparatus causing laryngeal and pharyngeal damage. One should refrain, as far as possible, from imitating another's voice.

J

Judgement and Judiciousness

Judgement and judiciousness are of prime importance for voice users in general. Poor judgement will result in attempts at vocal acrobatics beyond one's capability, resulting in voice damage.

K

Key

The key to a brilliant and perfect voice is balance. Balance all aspects of your life – eating, drinking, exercising, sleeping, breathing and maintaining peace of mind.

L

Laughter

Although laughter may be the best medicine for a world of illnesses, excessive laughter can irritate and inflame the vocal cords. Take care. Laugh, but not too much or too loudly.

Learning of Techniques

For the best results, you need to learn techniques to improve your breathing, modulating, voicing and projecting the voice. This learning curve is a continuous process as one gradually achieves perfection over time. One strives to internalize these techniques so that they come into play intuitively.

Loudness

Loudness is a very important aspect for a professional voice user. Amplification can be developed by using good breathing techniques and increasing lung power with exercises.

Loving Your Voice

Like the rest of your body, you need to love your voice, nurture it, care for it and use it well. If you hate your voice, it is highly doubtful whether you are going to be successful at it.

M

Microphone

If you are addressing a crowd or if the ambient noise levels are high, insist on a microphone. Even if you are singing at an impromptu party, picnic or small function, always insist on it. Not only does your voice sound good, it prevents you from straining your voice.

Monitor

As with all the other parameters of the body, the voice too needs to be monitored closely. Voice abnormalities are one of the prime symptoms for deeper, underlying problems. Therefore, take action immediately in the form of voice rest or visit your doctor.

N

Noise

Noise is one of the biggest enemies of voice. Noise pollution in the environment will impel you to shout and raise your voice in order to be heard. This places a lot of strain on your voice. Be aware of noise and avoid shouting when the environment is noisy.

Need for Talk

Talk only when you need to, not because you have to. Most actors and singers of repute spend a large part of their day in silence. Talking incessantly and unnecessarily should be avoided, as it strains the voice.

O

Opening Up

As a person, for the voice to open up, you too need to open up as well. A narrow-minded person with a closed consciousness will emit low volume and have a choked voice.

Opening Your Mouth

If you open your mouth fully and speak, your pronunciation will be much better and your voice will be louder too.

Originality

There is no substitute for the original and your voice is your very own unique identity. Treasure it and strengthen it. Don't imitate or copy anyone. In addition to straining the voice, going Hollywood makes you sound dreadfully fake.

P

Pollution

Air pollution is on the increase in every modern city across the world, more so in Third World countries where legislations against pollution are not as stringent as in developed countries. Toxic gases and noxious fumes can ruin the voice. Keep away from highly polluted environments. Wear a mask if required. Take frequent breaks to visit unpolluted places to give your voice some succour.

Pitch

Your pitch is unique to you and is technically called your fundamental frequency. If you speak or sing at your natural pitch, your voice will sound good and will take the least effort. It will also avoid any damage to the vocal cords. Try and find your pitch; understand, recognize and stick to it as far as possible.

Q

Quiet

Quiet or silence happens when you take voice rest. This is another very important tool to maintain a good voice. The more you rest your voice and stay quiet, the better your voice will be.

R

Range

Every human being has a voice range above and below his natural pitch. Exceeding this normal range requires voice-building exercises. If done without proper preparation, it is a recipe for disaster and could cause irreparable damage to the voice apparatus.

Rest

Voice rest is being repeated as I cannot stress enough on how crucial this is for optimum vocal performance.

S

Sleep

A good night's sleep, of at least eight hours, can do wonders for even a strained voice. When we sleep, our body repairs its tissues, including any minor damage to the voice apparatus that may have occurred during the day. Lack of sleep causes tiredness and increases acidity, both of which are not good for the voice. A good night's sleep also relaxes the body and mind, which will help your voice sound fresh and enthusiastic. Resting the body with sensible bed times is essential for maintaining the voice in its best condition.

Struggle

Whenever you feel that you are struggling with your voice – stop. Don't continue whatever vocal activity you are doing – speaking, shouting or singing – if you feel the pressure building up; let it go!

T

Tiredness

Any sort of tiredness, whether of the body, mind or voice, is a sign to take a break from whatever you are doing. 'Don't flog a dead horse' is a good idiom to remember.

Time

The human voice sounds and feels different at different times of the day. The time that your voice is at its freshest and most energetic is when you should practise your song or speech.

U

Understanding

It is mandatory that you are clear about the dynamics, anatomy, physiology and mechanics of the vocal infrastructure, and understand what improves or aggravates your voice. Otherwise, you will be unable to get the optimum results with your voice.

V

Voice Rest

Once again, the importance of voice rest cannot be emphasized enough. Whenever possible, give your voice a rest. Go on a twelve- or twenty-four-hour 'maun vrat' or no-speech period, once in a while, to protect and preserve your voice.

Value

Value your voice, for it is of the utmost importance in your repertoire as a voice-using professional. Don't neglect, take for granted, abuse or do stupid things with your voice unless you have trained it well. Do your warm-ups, cool-downs and daily exercises; don't forget to take enough voice rest.

W

Warm-ups

Warms-ups are a very important aspect of voice care. Like every physical activity or sport, the voice user needs to warm up, just as athletes do, to avoid injury or cramps. Please refer to the warm-up exercises section in the chapter titled 'The Complete Vocal Exercise Guide'.

X

eXcellence

To achieve excellence in your voice performance, understand your voice and be one with it. Live for the moment, be cheerful and light-hearted and do your exercises conscientiously. Take time out to listen to all the great professionals and observe how they use their voices. Find a good voice coach who will help you take care of your voice. Drink plenty of fluids, eat in moderation and take lots of voice rest. Follow all the techniques mentioned in this book to perfect yourself and achieve a great voice.

Z

Zest, Zip, Zing

If you want a voice which has a lot of zest, zip and zing, you need to bring these qualities into your personal life. Your voice ultimately reflects your personality, your feelings and moods, fears and anxieties, dreams and aspirations, even your barriers and obstinacies. Be free, open up, develop a passion for using your voice, practise, observe, imbibe and hear your voice grow zestful, full of life and warmth, becoming a magnet which draws the audience and makes them want more.

Having covered all the scientific and physical aspects of the voice, I would like to talk about something which is very close to my heart: a technique which I have used with several clients with very successful results. It is about using the power of your mind, thought and energy to address some of the issues you may have with your voice. So read on!

14

THE PSYCHOLOGY OF VOICE

What Your Voice Is Telling You

We have explored and understood the various scientific aspects of voice, how it is produced, how your breath is the main support system for it, the parameters of voice, and how we need to improve these parameters to generate a good, booming, resonant voice. We have also gone through other aspects like diction, accents, modulation, endurance and projection, and performed some exercises to bring about an all-round improvement and strength in our voices. After having dealt with voice at a physical level, let's now try and understand it at a psychological and emotional level.

Most of us use our voice daily, without thinking too much about it. Little do we realize that our voice is a wonderful gift from God. Each of us has been blessed with a unique voice, much like our face and fingerprints. Our voice is often our first line of identity, especially in today's world, when our contact with someone is often over the telephone, before we actually meet and talk to them face to face. Nowadays, since a lot of communication takes place predominantly over the phone, don't you think you should feel good about your voice and focus more on it? After all, we really don't know how many deals, how many relationships went awry, after the other person heard our voice and judged us prematurely.

In today's world, with the explosion of email and WhatsApp chat and instant messaging services, we are using our voices less and less. This is actually a big disadvantage, because our voice lets us inject energy into our thoughts

and lends more of our personality into what we want to convey. A text or an email, although convenient and quick, often strips the communication of emotion or feeling. The moment we use our voice, the emotion in it more effectively puts across what we're saying, and does it way better than an email or a text message. Electronic communication – and even written communication on paper – over the years, deprived man of an important means of communication: of using his voice.

Having said this, let us actually explore the mental and psychological aspects related to voice. In the human body, the voice box – or larynx – is placed at the throat. To be sure, it actually lies between the heart and the head. And it is powered by breath, which comes from deep inside the lungs (located close to the heart) and gets pushed out through the larynx, which vibrates, and the air column resonates in various chambers, before coming out. What this means is that our voice is a tool which connects our head to our heart; it is literally the meeting place of both. Both contribute equally to the voice, and what we speak or express is – or should be – an ideal mixture of emotions, which come from the heart, and rational thinking, intellect and logic, which come from the head. Lately though, the heart component of the voice has been somewhat silenced, and what we speak is mostly from the head. We are now conditioned and domesticated in our use of words and language – the result is that most of us have lost our 'signature' voice – something that seems more genuine – which we probably possessed centuries ago.

We can use our voice to express so many things – laughter, joy, squeals of delight, the agony of sorrow, the moans and groans of illness, the cry of helplessness, the shriek of horror or fear, humming a tune, coughing, sneezing, yawning – all these convey so much information and feelings without uttering a word. Truly, the human voice is a superb device that can achieve so much for us, if we learn to use it properly, speak from the heart and speak the truth.

We often underestimate the impact our voice can create. With enough power, opera singers can raise the pitch of their voices to a frequency high enough to shatter glass. When we speak loudly or angrily, our voices can cause much physical and mental agony to others. Likewise, we could decide to use our voices soothingly, lovingly, with affection, care and compassion, to love, bond, to forgive and ask for forgiveness, or to encourage, inspire, motivate, negotiate, plead, and even to heal. The power of our voices is such that a lawyer can even use it effectively to get an accused acquitted. A doctor could convincingly talk to a patient and make him understand and agree to surgery or a different form of treatment. A salesman could easily charm potential customers with his voice and make them buy stuff they may not actually need. A teacher, with her voice, could ignite the minds of young ones, and inspire them to pursue their goals and ambitions.

A CEO can use his voice persuasively to crack a deal, or to motivate his staff to perform better. A lover can express his love for his beloved and make her feel in seventh heaven. Used harshly, it could break off the relationship and send both into emotional hell. A strong voice is mandatory in certain professions, like those employed with the armed forces or the police. A drill sergeant with a dull, thin, low-pitched voice is unlikely to command much respect from his subordinates. A police officer's voice should send a chill up a criminal's spine and make him shudder. Even to control animals like dogs or horses, one needs to have a commanding voice and needs to show his control, not through violent actions, but through the power of his voice. The same is true for parents, when dealing firmly with children.

Our voice is the outward expression of our life force, our energy. Hence, by listening to someone's voice carefully, we can pick up the nuances which go beyond words that are being spoken, and can understand the reality of the person who is speaking. Much of our day-to-day programming and conditioning, our beliefs, our truths, our worries and anxieties, our fears and desires, our guilt and our anger, as well as our hopes and aspirations, are all imprinted on our subconscious mind. Normally, our speech and communication is dependent on our conscious mind. However, the subconscious has a constant but subtle effect on the conscious mind. The subconscious mind doesn't lie, and presents only the facts. The conscious mind, however, can choose to tell the truth, to hide it, to skirt it, or to disguise it. But because we are eventually drawing our energy from our subconscious – the same energy which drives our heart, our breathing, our circulation, digestion, excretion – we cannot really tell a lie without the subconscious programme intervening in some way or the other.

This is true of posture, body language and voice. When a person talks what he truly believes to be the truth, his voice is steady, firm and confident. When a person is either hiding the truth or disguising it, his voice and his facial movements tend to give it away. The eyes often look downward and a person speaking a lie cannot look another person in the eye. He also is likely to fidget with his hands, cross his legs, move his hands over his hair, or exhibit some mannerism which is an effort to cover the lie, physically.

Likewise, the voice, when speaking a lie – unless one is an established actor or an accomplished liar – often falters, becomes low, weak, becomes low- or high-pitched and has a lot of 'aahs' and 'umms' and pauses. The flow of speech is never as smooth when you are telling a lie, as it is with the truth. Try as hard as you want, and you will always find a difference. I urge you to experiment and try it out yourself. Next time you are talking to someone, try and listen to your voice (or that of the other person) when the truth is being spoken, and when the truth is being hidden or distorted. You can try and say a simple sentence like 'I am a man' and 'I am a woman'. If you are a man, and you say you are a man, your voice will be unwavering and solid. When you lie and say that you are a woman, your voice cannot have the same conviction and strength, because the energy which is feeding your speech is coming from your subconscious mind deep down, and the subconscious can distinguish between the truth and lies.

The same principle is used in muscle testing, to test a subconscious belief. A person is asked to hold out his arm straight. Pressure is applied on his arm to push it down. He is then asked leading questions. If he speaks the truth, the arm remains strong and cannot be easily pushed down. If he speaks a lie, the arm goes limp and can easily be pushed down. This approach is true for our voice as well. It tends to weaken and falter when the truth – or what we believe to be the truth – is not spoken. Many other parameters also change when a lie is spoken, e.g. the heartbeats, breathing rate and blood pressure. These parameters are used in standard polygraph or lie detector tests to determine the veracity of a statement.

The purpose of describing all the above is to make the reader realize that very often, as an actor, singer, teacher or lawyer, you might be going through a lot of personal issues in life. The human voice is also subject to change in many day-to-day situations, like after a flight, or during menstruation, or after menopause, not to mention during illnesses like cold, cough and other ailments. As a professional who depends on a good voice for livelihood, you need to be aware of these changes, and factor them in prior to a performance. For example, performing on-stage immediately after a long flight may not bring out the best in your voice. Likewise, rumour has it that many famous opera singers and performers made sure that their contracts stated that they would not sing or perform when they were on their period, as the voice often becomes thick and inflexible.

Many of us also wear what is called a 'voice mask'. We are all born with our own voice, much like our fingerprints, which is unique and our own. But as we discussed earlier, due to various conditionings and needs, we tend to hide our original voice, and often cultivate a false or a pseudo voice in our daily life. Cultivating a special voice for your profession is fine, as we need to give our best for our professional ventures. But as a human being, your voice needs to reflect who you are, what your aspirations are, and what you stand for and believe. When we carry this 'voice mask' on to our normal daily voices, it becomes a cloak of sorts, with which we cover our real selves, and often get frustrated and restless, simply because we cannot truly express ourselves.

Every human being is born with the need to express himself or herself, starting with a newborn baby who begins to cry and fuss uncontrollably the moment it's born. As we grow older, we feel the need to portray to the world who we are and what we want. But many of us tend to hide our real voices in order to sound acceptable in society. If this continues over a period of time, it could cause a lot of internal conflict and result in a lot of emotional issues. Using a false voice mask makes you frustrated, and a negative vicious cycle is set up, from which it becomes difficult to step out, unless you are able to unravel all the threads of this mystery.

While we know that disease obviously makes us weak and infirm and will change our voice, what we don't realize is that many emotional issues – guilt, anger, apathy, frustration, restlessness, worry, anxiety, desire, fear, jealousy, resentment, past traumas, childhood abuse – can affect the voice. Many a time, I have clients with choked voices who come to me for therapy. On examination, I've often found that nothing is wrong with their vocal apparatus. But they sound very strained. Probing further, it becomes obvious that they are under severe emotional distress and are often not able to freely express themselves at home or at work, and this leads to a stifled voice. Similarly, some clients complain about pain every time they speak and deeper questioning reveals that they are experiencing some personal issues which they would rather not talk about. The physical or emotional pain doesn't take long to translate into in their voice.

As we end this chapter, it is pertinent to note that many voice related ailments are related to our state of mind. Here is a short list of voice and speech conditions, and some possible mental or psychological correlations which I've derived from my years of practice and experience. Many of my clients have found tremendous improvement in their voices by dealing with other aspects of their lives.

- Unclear diction is often an indicator of imprecise or confused thought processes.
- Overemphatic speech is often a sign of lack of trust and pushing outwardly.
- Unclear word endings and not pronouncing the words fully are often an indication of not being present totally, and of not thinking completely, and also may indicate fear of responsibility and fear of authority.
- A stiff jaw or stiff lips indicates an unwillingness to communicate and may arise from mistrust.
- Staccato speech often happens in people who are scared of feeling.
- Lazy or slow speech is sign of powerlessness.
- Anxiety often causes a glottal attack or a feeling of speech being stuck in the throat.
- A monotonous, flat voice is often an indication of depression or extreme boredom.

Generally, the most common problem people face is that of hoarseness, or loss of voice, something that usually happens once you're back home from a picnic, or after too much shouting and singing. A hoarse voice or a sore voice is often a result of physical strain, on the physical level. But on a psychological level, it means that we are trying to say many things, but holding back because of fear of being ridiculed, or fear of rejection, or fear of authority, or simply, a fear of making a fool of ourselves. Often, if we have to make a request which we feel is likely to be turned down, we tend to hold back our words, which changes our voice. Instead, we need to be clear, calm and freely express ourselves without fear or worry. Or else, with suppression, we will land up initially with voice problems, and eventually with many other physical and psychological ailments.

With this, we have now come to the end of section one of this book. We now move on to the second section, which deals with voice in specific situations and for specific people.

PART TWO

SPECIFIC CONCEPTS

Which Basic Elements to Use, and How Much?

1

THE ACTOR'S VOICE

Indians are passionate about two things – cricket and films. I am no exception. Fortunately, a large part of my work involves voice training for upcoming and established actors in the Indian film industry. Having worked with them for over twenty years, and also having created and taught curricula for voice training in various acting schools, it gives me great pleasure to write this chapter.

The voice is almost like a body part of an actor, and it is subject to a lot of stress and strain. Cinema is a visual medium and although a large part of audience attention is on the visuals, the manner in which voice and speech come together for dialogue delivery is of immense importance. It can actually make or break a performance.

I cannot over-emphasize the importance of having a great voice, with all its components of flexibility, range, diction, accent, modulation, projection and endurance for an actor as this could be a point of contention when people consider you for a role in a film. If you're an aspiring actor, I don't want this to be the reason why you don't land a desired role or a film. Certain roles make very high demands of your vocal performance. And you might miss out on such roles if you are not perfect in your vocal skills. An example would be a film where you have a dual role – you play both father and son, or the role of twins. Or where the entire storyline rests on the shoulder of this character, like it does in biopics.

For actors, if you are good in everything else – dance, acting, fight scenes –but not in your voicing skills, a dubbing artist may come to your aid. This isn't a great sign, and personally, I don't prefer this at all, as I believe that God has given us the perfect voice to suit our physique, face and personality and it is near impossible to match it up with someone else's voice.

So, every time your voice is dubbed by someone else, there will always be a mismatch and something will feel amiss. So as an actor, you need to ask yourself: when you work so hard on your acting skills, work out to regularly to have a great body, develop excellent dancing and action skills, why wouldn't you work on achieving exemplary voicing skills? For example, great legends like Dilip Kumar, Amitabh Bachchan, Shabana Azmi, Rekha, etc., always had exceptional voicing skills, as part of their repertoire.

So here's what you need to do:

DEVELOP A SOLID VOICE

An actor's voice is part of his persona. He needs to develop a good breathing technique and also improvise and create a booming and resonant voice. Do revisit these two chapters in Section One of this book and to understand why a good voice is a solid foundation for any actor.

WORK ON DICTION AND ACCENTS

Having perfect pronunciation skills is also of utmost importance. Hence it's crucial to work on getting the diction absolutely spot on. A detailed step-by-step method is described in the chapter on diction. Perfecting diction could take several months of constant practice and is not an easy task by any standards. Coming to accents, you should ideally have a neutral accent in the language of the film. But if you have a hangover of your mother tongue, or from a language you frequently converse in, then the character you are playing in the movie will tend to get an accent which is not in keeping with its personality and the result will sound very odd to viewers. For example, if you're cast as a poor north Indian farmer in a Hindi film, and your accent sounds Tamil or Bengali, audiences will find it difficult to accept it. The disconnect will impact how the film is received by them. Working on your accent may often require you to take the services of a voice coach or a voice trainer.

WORK ON VOICE ENDURANCE

Since voice usage for an actor is often to extreme degrees, preserving its authenticity, preventing any disorders and maintaining its quality for long periods of time is of paramount importance. While acting and dubbing for a film, actors are often required to speak their dialogues for hours on end, and dialogue delivery is not easy: it involves shouting, screaming, whispering, reciting non-stop monologues – even repeating them over and over again – while doing a number of re-takes. On most occasions, the re-takes might not be his fault, but due to the shortcomings of his co-stars or crew members. He may even have to repeat his scenes over and over again, for a film shoot that usually lasts for many months.

Also, many established actors do more than one film at a time, and are constantly required to be present for promotions and publicity for their films by giving interviews and addressing audiences. All this usually leads an actor's voice to become terribly stressed and strained. Which is why, vocal endurance, or the ability to go on and on without sounding tired or weak, and without damaging one's vocal chords, is a very important part of an actor's training, and has to be maintained life-long. It is extremely important that the actor adopt a very good regime of vocal endurance exercises, good breathing techniques and develop regular vocal hygiene, so that he can meet the demands his profession makes of his voice.

VOICE PROJECTION

Many a time, actors have to yell, scream and 'throw' their voice. That's when their voice projection skills come into play. This is especially relevant for theatre actors because most theatre stages don't have good microphones and to be audible, the director has to rely heavily on actors. For good voice projection, one needs to work on breathing and posture – these are dealt with in the chapter on voice projection.

VOICE MODULATION

Probably the most important vocal technique one needs to develop, it is only through modulation that actors can let the emotions in their voice match their facial expressions and body language. This isn't an easy task by any standards, especially since actors may not be feeling those emotions at the time of enacting it. All of us express our feelings using our voice, but for us, emotion comes first and voice modulation automatically follows. For example, if I'm angry, I don't have to think about raising my pitch, or volume – these go up automatically as the anger guides me to do those things. Whereas as an actor, you may or may not feel those emotions in your heart, but you still have to express it through your voice. That is why understanding, learning and practising various modulation techniques is very important. So you must learn to explore the dynamic use of pitch, intonation, rhythm, rate, volume, pause and stress to create various emotions and be highly expressive. One needs to study the role, the text, make the sub-text in your script and scene work, and evolve a modulation plan to be carried out during the filming and dubbing. These techniques are described in detail in the chapter on voice modulation.

Often, actors play characters that are very different from who they are, in terms of cultural background, age, educational background and these are the times when modulation becomes a challenge, unless well-rehearsed.

COME UP WITH YOUR OWN PRE-PERFORMANCE WARM-UP ROUTINE

Pre-performance warm-up prevents vocal damage and increases your flexibility just the way athletes warm up before a race or a match. These are given in detail in the chapter on vocal endurance. As an actor, I urge you to never skip warm-ups as the demands on your voice are going to be exceptionally high.

DUBBING

There are two more aspects which are very specific to actors and which have not been mentioned in section one. One of them is dubbing. Earlier, all movies were dubbed – after the movie had been filmed, actors went to the dubbing studio to re-record all the dialogues. These days, many films use a technique called 'sync sound', wherein the voice is also captured along with the visuals and used in the final output. Still, there are many movies that continue to use dubbing. Let us explore a few aspects of dubbing.

First, the pace at which the dialogues are spoken and pauses taken during filming have to be replicated in dubbing. So, one has to have a plan of pacing and pausing while filming itself, and that has to be repeated during dubbing. For example, if you have spoken too fast with very few pauses during filming, there is no scope to do that during dubbing. Otherwise there won't be any lip sync at all. Having the right kind of modulation from the filming stage itself is of utmost importance. In a way, going back to the dubbing studio only gives you another chance to perform better in your voicing skills. Loudness and pitch variations can be added later, while dubbing. Your diction and accents can also be improved while dubbing, if not done appropriately during filming. Even the quality of your voice, voice projection, etc., can all be worked upon during dubbing. So, although you can inject more life and emotion into your voice, you cannot change the pacing and the pausing of the voice.

More on dubbing: Sometimes, your voice and dialogues can get dubbed by another person if your producers and directors feel that your voicing skills are not good enough, they might call in a professional dubbing artist to do your lines. This happens to many actors in the initial stage of their career. I'm not particularly supportive of the idea – however good the dubbing artist may be, there is a disconnect and the audience can easily spot that something is amiss. I think every actor should dub their own lines as this creates a more sincere connect with viewers. So do your homework, work very hard on your voice and voicing skills – let's say, for six to eight months before your shoot – and ensure that you dub in your own voice.

VOICE STYLING

This is the second aspect about actors and it's a concept which is very dear to me. Just like you recreate the physical aspects of the character that you are playing, be it clothes, physique, hair, looks, mannerisms, body language, etc., you need to create a specific voice style for each character that you are playing. It would depend on the age, the educational status, background (cultural and financial) of the character. Based on this, you can create a specific style of voice, accent and modulation.

For example, if you are playing a villager, you will speak in a certain way. If you are playing an NRI, you will introduce a slight foreign accent in your speech. One example that instantly comes to my mind is actor Tom Hanks, who almost always has a totally different voice in every movie. In *Terminal*, we saw him with a very nasal, high-pitched voice and an east European accent, whereas in *Forrest Gump*, he had a very low-pitched voice and lengthy pacing. Kamal Hassan is another master of voice styling; he masterfully incorporates cultural and character-driven variations into each character. In *Michael Madana Kamarajan*, he played four brothers, each having totally different voices, accent, diction and modulation. In *Chachi 420*, Kamal Hassan actually sounded like an elderly woman and he was almost flawless. Govinda has done voice styling in *Haseena Maan Jaayegi*, where he plays both uncle and nephew. Also, who can forget Amitabh Bachchan's impressive voice styling in *Agneepath*, *Aakhree Raasta*, *Paa* and *Piku*? It didn't mean just the change in accent and diction, but at times, changing the very nature of his voice, in terms of pitch, loudness and resonance.

To summarize, here's what I recommend:

- Have a voice profile as per your character. Determine what pitch, loudness and resonance you want to use.
- Have a diction and accent profile.
- Have a general modulation profile – for example, be clear about whether you are a loud character, or a soft spoken one, etc.
- In each scene, analyse your emotions, and have a modulation profile for that scene and then use the tools given in the voice modulation chapter to execute it.

2

THE NEWS PRESENTER'S VOICE

144 When one listens to the news, what does one want to experience? For starters, one wants to hear a strong, commanding voice which sounds good on the ears. Sure, the news itself has to be interesting, but apart from that, one wants to listen to clear and crisp diction and pronunciation. Also, one would prefer a neutral accent, and would not like to see other accents getting carried forward into the news.

When I did my first training programme for news anchors, I was rather surprised to know that these anchors were selected based on their journalistic skills and not on their presentation skills. As a result, their news presentation left a lot to be desired. The CEO of the organization had his task cut out for me: I was to train these newscasters and improve their presenting skills.

As a news presenter, you are primarily concerned about content. But how you present it is also extremely important. As I was training the news presenters and speaking to them about presenting the news in an interesting way, some of them joked and told me that audiences responded more to well-presented news, rather than the content itself! Though this was an overstatement – and we all know that content is of paramount importance – presentation is of equal value. In fact, I told them that content could guide them to form better presentation strategies.

The most important aspect of news reading is voice modulation. Although there is an earlier section on voice modulation, there are a few aspects that I would like to elaborate here. Voice modulation means different things for different people. For an actor, it helps bring out the emotions. For a singer, it helps produce melody. For a teacher, it means authority and helps impart knowledge about a specific subject. For a news anchor, modulation means explaining core issues to the viewer clearly, expressing their gravity, and holding the attention of audiences by making the content interesting. As I said earlier, content is king, and certain matters are interesting by the very nature of the content. And presentation skills actually become secondary. But certain segments are not very interesting, like weather reports, market research, politics, social reforms, etc., and this is where the presentation skills come in handy.

Here are a few steps that you can take to modulate your voice:

- Go over your content and categorize them as formal versus casual, serious versus light, and mandatory versus non-mandatory.
- While you do so, mark the most important word in every sentence.
- This highlighted word would change depending on whether your content is formal or casual, serious or light, etc.
- Stress on the particular word that you have kept in your mind and keep the rest of the sentence natural. For example, if you were to say 'Today is an extremely hot day', you would obviously stress on 'extremely'.
- In some perspectives, stressing on a particular word can change the meaning of what you are trying to say but not in news presentation. So, don't worry, relax, if you do happen to stress on words that are not so important, no big deal. But, it does change the perspective of what you are trying to say. For example, if you say: 'The markets have fallen by 300 points in just one hour', by stressing on 'the markets', there is going to be no major impact on what you are saying. But, if instead you stressed on the words '300' and 'one hour', the impact that you will create in the mind of the listener is tremendous.

- Research has shown that audiences like to hear certain news readers, day after day and month after month, even if that person is not on a preferred news channel, or if that particular news channel does not have very good visuals, bytes, or tickers. Research has also shown that the way things are said from this preferred newsreader has more impact on the audiences' mind. Viewers even depend on information given by certain preferred anchors to decide when and where to invest their money. Although content about the stock markets is more or less the same across all news channels, viewers prefer to listen to and follow one or two of their favourite presenters, only because of the way they present this content.

- If content is casual, then the number of words you stress on will be much less. For example, if you were to look at these sentences about the automobile sector performance: 'The last quarter has seen a drastic drop in automobile sales. The mid-priced segment is the strongest. The high-priced segment has seen the maximum fall. And the luxury segment has almost recorded no sales. The reasons could be the fact that it is the last quarter of the financial year and an unstable market.'

If you read out these lines without stressing on any word or words, it would still sound reasonably fine. Or if you just stressed on 'drastic drop', then too the matter gets across.

Whereas, if the content was formal, like: 'This national election has seen a major sweep by the Congress party which has got a huge majority of eighty percent of the seats. The reasons cited are a sympathy wave due to the death of a prominent personality and also poor performance by the previous government.'

The above lines would require you to stress on a lot of words like 'major sweep', 'huge', 'eighty', 'sympathy', 'death' and 'poor performance'. If you did not do this, the impact of what you are trying to say would be totally lost. So, all that I am trying to tell you is to understand your content really well, categorize it, mark the key words, say it over and over in your mind, and see for yourself if you are able to create the impact that the content is supposed to create and is capable of creating.

- Headlines and politics form formal stuff. Weather is casual.
- Serious and light could be similar to formal and casual. Serious news would involve national calamities, crimes, acts of terrorism, and outbreaks of epidemics. Light would be about sports, fashion or wildlife. These topics would require the same treatment of formal versus casual with a few minor variations. For example, hard news such as serious crimes, terrorism or natural calamities would require a lot more punctuations and keyword stresses than formal news. The other difference would be that these issues involve a lot more emotions as compared to other formal events. So, there will be an emotional wave (positive or negative) riding along with it. The two aspects that need to be looked in here are:
- The news presenter needs to project the right sentiment, which means stressing on the wrong words can have a negative impact. For example, 'The whole nation is mourning the ghastly terrorist act of the murder of the

Prime Minister by a human bomb.' If you did not stress on any word, it would sound as if you were not bothered, but if you stressed on 'whole', 'ghastly', 'terrorist' and 'Prime Minister' it would sound appropriate, as the presenter is also showing a bit of anger, shock and concern. But if he stressed on 'the human bomb', it would sound as if he was giving prime importance to the human bomb. So, it's important to think about the content, the emotions and try out various stress points and then go with the feeling that viewers are likely to experience. If you are truly feeling the emotions as any normal human being, these things would come naturally to you. But it does not mean that if you are not emotionally attached that you cannot read the news; you just have to be particular about how you sound. And it is perfectly alright for you not to be emotionally attached to every issue.

- Having stated the above, it is also crucial not to portray any strong personal emotion as you read out the news. It is a tough game, of being there and not being there. You need to be able to make an impact, but try and sound as objective and non-judgmental as possible.
- Many times, as an anchor, you are also a moderator for group discussions. These require totally different modulation skills and voice skills. The first voice skill you require here is to have a loud and commanding voice, as panellists in such groups tend to get unruly at times. Let's take a look at the following example, where you will note the importance of being non-accusatory:

> 'The current situation warrants you as the Chief Police Commissioner of the city to take strong and stern action against the miscreants. The fact that the miscreants are prominent and powerful people should not alter your sense of justice.'

If you stressed on 'you' and 'alter your', it would sound very accusatory. Whereas if you stressed on 'chief police', 'strong and stern' and 'sense of justice', it would sound non- accusatory, but at the same time, it would drive home the point.

Meanwhile, as a sports anchor or a commentator, various other aspects come into play. If you look at it in simplistic terms, you are just conveying what is happening on the ground. It is a commentary. If it is for radio, where there are no visuals, it is pretty simple, as you just keep giving an account of what exactly is happening on the ground and that would take away most of your time and energy. If it is for television, you are aided by a lot of visuals. Often, you also act as an analyst, and you have to give your opinions and predictions as well. You have to guard against getting emotionally attached to any one team. You keep the modulations limited to stressing on keywords, and comment on what is happening. Your challenge will be on the days when the events are really boring, and you need to keep up the attention of the audiences. Of course, content will continue to guide you about what key words to emphasize. As with the news presenter, you need to be non-judgemental, non-accusatory, keep it interesting and hold the audience's attention.

The various ways of doing modulation, by varying the parameters of your pitch, resonance, loudness, stress, pause, tone, intonation etc., are dealt with in great detail in the chapter on voice modulation.

So, go ahead, modulate your voice and read your stuff, so that people are hooked to you and turn on their television sets, at your time.

3

THE LAYPERSON'S VOICE

The number of professional voice artists in the world is very small. If you are not an actor, singer, a theatre person, a corporate executive, a teacher, a lawyer, etc., you use your voice predominantly for communicating mundane, day-to-day issues with people. Your use of voice is restricted to home, office and public places. You need to have a good voice and you need a voice to be able to communicate well and to make yourself understood. Hence, it is also likely that you really don't think about your voice at all, and use it with as much awareness and ease as you do with breathing, circulation, digestion, eating, sleeping, etc. Your voice is never a big deal. You are a common man who needs a normal voice, not an extraordinary one.

Then why have we included this chapter in this book? Since the common man almost never thinks about his voice and uses it as he pleases – he almost never undergoes any voice training, for that matter – his voice is prone to much damage. Moreover, since he is unaware, he continues to use his voice even when it is damaged, often leading to major voice problems, sometimes even requiring medication or surgery. Once he is cured, unless he takes care, he goes back to his old ways, only to go back to the doctor, with a hoarse voice. For some people, a hoarse voice becomes a recurrent issue, with no cure in sight.

What are the situations in which the common man abuses or misuses his voice, which is untrained and much prone to damage? Here are a few situations:

- Mothers and fathers screaming at their children to keep up the discipline at home
- Partners and/or spouses having a yelling match at home during a conflict
- Children having major arguments with parents
- Shouting at subordinates, or juniors, or at salesmen or domestic help for not doing their job properly
- Getting upset at the mall, or on the road, or picking up a fight with someone at the pub and yelling
- Cheering at any sports event or show
- Singing once in a while at parties or at gatherings
- Singing in chorus without practice – choir singing or singing bhajans at a religious venue
- Screaming and playing at picnics

Most of us have gone through a hoarse voice after at least one of the above situations. After taking medication for a few days, we're usually okay. But in some cases, since we continue talking in spite of a voice injury, our voice does not improve and worsens instead. On consulting a specialist, we are told that we have vocal damage or vocal nodules, and we are treated initially with medicines, and occasionally with surgery.

As a voice therapist, it is easier for me to convince a professional voice user than someone who is not one to safeguard his voice or practise vocal hygiene. The professional voice user is usually a very cooperative client because his livelihood depends on it. But I often struggle with the common man, who takes it very lightly and often refuses to follow my instructions, and keeps coming back with some excuse or the other for not following instructions.

Hence I felt it is a good idea to include a chapter on the common man and his voice so that you will realize the pitfalls of taking your voice and your voice problems lightly.

Your voice is a part of your personality, and irrespective of whether you are using it to talk to your kids, converse with your partner, bargain at the local market, or chat to someone at a party, if your voice is harsh, hoarse, gravelly, inaudible, nasal, or if you are struggling to speak and hurting, it does affect the quality of your life. And if you do go for a job interview, the poor state of your voice might jeopardize your chances of landing the job. This is especially true for jobs where there is a client interface, like a receptionist, or a telephone operator or a front-desk executive.

I can only say the same thing to the common man which I say to all the professional voice users. Your voice is an asset, it is part of your identity, it can make the difference between your commands being followed or ignored, can make the difference between people mistaking you for a strong, responsible person versus a weak, inefficient person. I would advise you to remember that your voice is valuable and to take good care of it, and not get into a shouting match, or cheering or singing occasionally without knowing that you are headed for danger.

Why should you not also read the chapters on diction, accent, voice modulation, endurance and projection and use your voice more effectively in your day to day situations? A good, commanding voice with pleasant modulation, perfect pronunciation, and neutral accent will only be an asset to you and bring gains in your personal and professional ventures. As we all spend time and energy in grooming ourselves to look good and dress well, voice should also become a part of grooming. Good communication skills will only bring you gains. So I encourage each and every person to work on his voicing and speaking skills, to enhance their life.

4

THE TEACHER'S VOICE

Teachers are probably the most underrated of all professional voice users and the most non-glamorous but they're a set of people with real and difficult issues. Also, unlike actors or singers who can finish their job and go on to relax and rest their voices, teachers don't have that luxury. They continue using their voices even when they are off duty.

In India, another problem comes up: monthly remuneration is poor and teachers take on more students for private tuitions and coaching in order to increase their income. Obviously, this only adds to their already strained vocal cords. The main problem is that they need to reach out to a large group of forty or fifty students (or even more) – who may or may not be interesting in being receptive in the first place – often without a microphone or a sound system in the classroom. Traditionally, teachers had to work with a blackboard and chalk, and the chalk dust tends to irritate the vocal cords and add to the voice problems. This, however, is changing nowadays as teachers are using more and more electronic methods to aid their teaching methods.

School teachers have another issue. They often deal with mischievous, noisy and unruly children, and apart from using their voices for teaching, they also have to shout and scream at them to maintain order and decorum. Talking to students for long hours is one thing; but screaming and shouting, even for brief periods, can be extremely damaging to the vocal cords.

In my many years of practice, I have closely worked with plenty of people in the teaching profession, and what I have found is that they reach out to me only when their voices have finally given up. Many of them said that they never knew that they needed to take care of their voice, or that it could be trained for effective usage.

The two important areas that teachers need to work on, in respect to their voices, are endurance and projection. Working on these two areas will actually prevent them from having any voice-related issues and will allow them to use their voice effectively for long periods of time. The one skill that they need to learn is to use the breath and coordinate their breathing while speaking so that there is no strain on the voice. Kindly refer to the chapter on breathing and vocal endurance for necessary guidance.

It is not possible for the teacher to remember all these nuances. They need to make it a part of their routine. They need to work on their breathing, vocal hygiene, warm-up regimes and establish a daily vocal exercise regime. It will also help her to incorporate weekly periods of voice rest as that would take care of the excesses that have happened during the week. The voice rest regime is probably the most important and voice saving step that a teacher needs to take. Basically, a teacher needs the following:

- Understand that he or she is using their voice more than permissible and also in ways that are not permissible.
- Realize that in the long run, there could be permanent vocal damage.
- Invest in good voice training skills like breathing and projection.
- Set up a daily vocal exercise and warm-up regime.
- Set up a weekly voice rest regime.

Last but not the least, he or she needs to be vigilant and at the first sign of any vocal trouble, visit a doctor or therapist, so that things can be set right at the earliest and permanent vocal damage can be prevented.

5

THE SINGER'S VOICE

Being a singer myself, I realize that singers require a lot more time and effort to develop a great voice, compared to any other professional voice user. If speaking is equivalent to walking, singing is akin to athletics and gymnastics. Singing is an activity that requires as much training, dedication and effort as the body requires for any sporting or athletic activity. All of us walk, jog, go to the gym and exercise our bodies for perhaps an hour or two; whereas a sportsperson or athlete probably puts in six to eight hours of workouts in order to excel in his sport. Training the voice for singing is comparable to this. In singing, one uses a much greater vocal range than what is used for speaking. We also perform complex vocal feats that we shall discuss later.

Knowledge of music, present in the brain, is transmitted to the vocal apparatus that serves as the instrument. For a musician, although every instrument does require some adjustment from time to time, it's a lot easier to harmonize a musical instrument than finetune the vocal cords. This instrument is extraordinary because, as a part of the body, it is susceptible to all bodily changes and illnesses. Unlike other instruments, it is also used for talking, crying, laughing and many other such activities apart from singing. Therefore, the vocal cords, viewed as an instrument, are rather unique, delicate, complex, sensitive and sorely overused. They also have a lot of physical restrictions unlike any other musical instrument. Furthermore, if a musical instrument like a guitar, flute or drum is defective, it can be replaced easily, whereas the vocal cords are a permanent fixture. Therefore, a singer belongs to one set of professional voice users who really need to work on voice training for maintenance, strength and stamina.

It is a fundamental fact that breathing is the lifeline for a singer. One not only has to develop deep breathing techniques but also use it effectively to sing. Singers have often been told, 'Sing from your stomach, not your throat.' This simply means coordinating the breath with vocalizing. As discussed in the chapter on breathing, when you fill your lungs with air, your diaphragm goes down and pushes your abdomen out, and when you exhale, the abdomen goes in. This happens if you fill your lungs fully with air, and that is what is called deep breathing. As this is a visible phenomenon with deep breathing, the phrase 'sing from your' abdomen has been coined and used by all singers and trainers.

Acquiring deep breathing is fairly easy and can be achieved with just a few days of practice. However, integrating it with singing is tough. Therefore, I shall provide a step-by-step method in the exercise plan later in this chapter. Without synchronizing one's singing and breathing (singing from the throat, in layman's terms), the output will be severely restricted. Harnessing the breath to sing provides the following benefits:

- Endurance, i.e., the ability to sing without tiring your voice for over two to three hours.
- Ability to reach the extreme ends of your vocal range, the lowest and highest notes, with ease.
- Having good volume at the extreme ends of your range, both lower and higher.
- Performing complex functions like the vibrato, gamaka, riff and falsetto.
- Modulating your voice with ease.

I reiterate that if one does not learn to use one's breath for singing, in the long run, vocal damage is inevitable for a singer. Singers are probably the people who are most prone to vocal troubles like hoarseness, vocal nodules, etc., all of which are preventable by learning to use the right technique.

The chapters on breathing, endurance, projection and why you should learn to sing are of utmost importance for the singer and I request you to include the exercises mentioned here into your daily routine.

Let's now discuss a few aspects of the singing voice.

IDEAL PITCH AND VOCAL RANGE

When we speak, we don't stop to wonder, 'Am I speaking at my ideal pitch?' It somehow comes naturally to us as we learn to speak. However, there are a few individuals who speak at the wrong pitch and eventually land up with a speech therapist, because speaking at the wrong pitch will inevitably lead to a lot of voice troubles and vocal fatigue. Finding one's ideal pitch is crucial for singing. When you begin your training in singing, your music teacher will guide you to find your ideal pitch. There are, however, many who do not have formal training in music and haven't the faintest idea about their ideal singing pitch. At this juncture, I would also like to tell you about another concept called octave, which comprises eight notes. In Indian music, they are: Sa, Re, Ga, Ma, Pa, Dha, Ni and Sa.

The ideal pitch is one where you can sing one octave and three or four notes on either side of the octave. Therefore, if you are singing at your ideal pitch, you should be able to sing one octave and take four notes in the sequential octaves at either end, with equal ease – Ma Pa Dha Ni *Sa Re Ga Ma Pa Dha Ni Sa* Re Ga Ma Pa. This is called your 'range' and even untrained voices have a range of one-and-a-half to two octaves. In a broader sense, the term 'vocal range' refers to the full spectrum of notes that a singer's voice is able to produce starting from the lowest and reaching the uppermost note. In other words, range refers to the distance between the highest and the lowest pitches that a singer is able to sing.

Pa Dha Ni	Sa Re Ga Ma Pa Dha Ni Sa	Re Ga Ma
Lower octave	Middle octave	Upper octave
	Total two octaves	

Often, a singer, unaware that he has more notes in his range than he knows about, restricts himself to only one style of singing. Music lessons and voice training can increase one's voice range by half an octave to one entire octave. Hence, a well-trained voice can have a range of up to three octaves. I urge you, therefore, to try out various pitches and find the most suitable pitch for you. This concept of ideal pitch is relevant and applicable to any form of music that you sing, be it Western or Indian, classical or jazz. Then again, it's not quite so simple because certain forms of singing, like opera, film music and Western music, use something called the falsetto or the head voice. Let us try and understand this by understanding the concept of 'registers'. Exercises to increase your range will be discussed later in the exercises section at the end.

REGISTERS

'Vocal register' is a term used for the range of your voice. In scientific terms, it means the various vibratory patterns your vocal cords are capable of producing. In layman's language, it is a series of pitches that you are capable of producing. The Indian and Western styles of music have their own terminologies and classifications for registers. Mainly, the vocal registers consist of the following six ranges:

- Vocal fry, the lowest

- The chest voice
- A mixed voice
- A head voice
- Falsetto
- Whistle

But to make things simple, I would like to divide it into just two components – a chest voice and a head voice. In the vocal range, the ideal pitch is a chest voice, where the entire larynx vibrates to produce this range. This is the voice used in Indian classical music. A head voice or falsetto is a higher pitch range where only the upper part of the vocal cords move, while the lower parts remain still. This voice is used a lot in Western music, opera singing and also in Indian film music.

Figure 5.1 shows how the vocal cords vibrate when we use the chest voice (left) and falsetto (right).

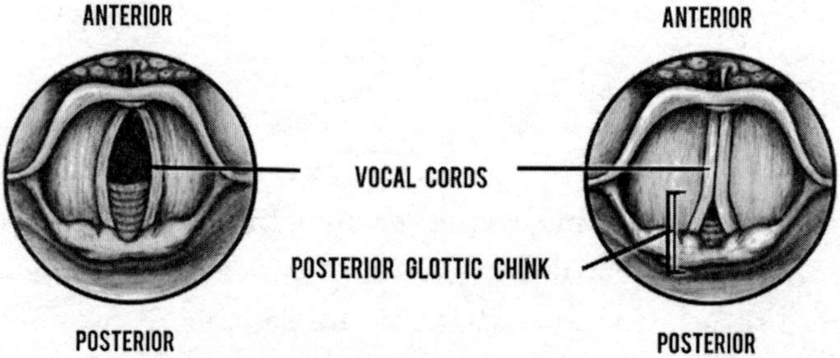

FIGURE 5.1: Laryngoscopy figures showing vibrations of vocal cords using chest voice and falsetto

Another aspect that needs to be trained is the transition between the two registers. A singer who learns both increases his range tremendously. Exercises to acquire various ranges, registers and transitions will be discussed later under the heading 'Exercises for singers'.

RESONANCE

As discussed in the chapter on the parameters of voice, resonance refers to the term of rotating the air in a particular part of your vocal tract more than in the rest. We also discussed three resonance patterns: throat resonance, mouth resonance and nasal resonance. The lower registers use more of throat resonance, the middle registers, oral resonance and the higher registers, nasal resonance. Therefore, I urge you to read the aforementioned chapter, particularly the section headed 'Resonance' and understand the concept better. Combining various registers with various resonance patterns can produce various tones and timbres of the voice. Every singer is actually capable of producing a variety of voices by understanding and training in these concepts. Resonance exercises is being discussed in the next section.

EXERCISES FOR SINGERS

Learning to Breathe Deep

Here is a step-by-step exercise guide to develop the ability to breathe deep:

- Get yourself into a quiet space. Switch off your phone.
- Lie supine with your head supported by a pillow and your spine as evenly aligned with the head as possible. Alternatively, you may sit cross-legged and erect. Ensure that you are wearing loose-fitting clothes that will allow your abdomen to move.
- Place one hand on your abdomen and the other on your chest.
- Inhale slowly, drawing in as much air as you possibly can until you are filled to capacity. You will notice that the chest and belly bulge outwards.
- Now slowly exhale and observe your chest and belly deflate.

- Ensure that your shoulders remain relaxed and still.
- The movement of the abdomen should not be upward towards the head, but it should move out towards the sky and then back in.
- Once you have completed one cycle of respiration (inhalation and exhalation), inhale for the next cycle.
- Do this for twelve counts before you take a break.
- Repeat the set of twelve deep breaths two more times.
- With time, you will be able to spontaneously take in more air with every breath.
- Over a period of time you will be doing deep breathing all the time.

Coordinating Breathing and Singing

One-note, one-breath singing

Take a slow deep breath and as you exhale, sing the first note 'Sa' at your pitch. Keep the singing loud so that by default you expel the air. There are two ways to become aware whether you are using your breath or not. Firstly, the voice will sound stronger and louder when you use your breath. Secondly, you will feel no pressure in the larynx. Gradually, you develop the ability to sense your exhalation and learn to coordinate it with your singing. Repeat this with all the notes in one octave and back – that is, Sa going up the scale to the eighth Sa and back. As soon as you are comfortable with this, reach out to the notes in the next octave above and the one below as follows:

Pa Dha Ni ... (Sa Re Ga Ma Pa Dha Ni Sa) ... Re Ga Ma

The notes within the parentheses represent your main octave. You have half an octave on either side, making your range two octaves.

This exercise will also help you determine your range. In due course, with practice, you will be able to further extend by one or two notes at either ends of your range. This exercise is done by taking a fresh breath for every single note.

Multiple notes

Take a long, deep breath and sing four notes as you exhale. Start at the lowest notes of your range and continue to the highest point. With practice the number of notes you can sing per breath will increase until you can cover the entire octave in a single breath.

Jumbled notes

Take a long, deep breath and practise singing various jumbled notes as you exhale. A few examples are:

- Sa Re Ga ... Re Ga Ma ... Ga Ma Pa ... Ma Pa Dha ... Pa Dha Ni ... Dha Ni Sa
- Sa Re ... Sa Ga ... Sa Ma ... Sa Pa ... Sa Dha ... Sa Ni ... Sa Sa

Repeat these in your entire vocal range. The idea of doing jumbled and multiple notes is to slowly shift your focus from breathing to singing, simultaneously ensuring that breath coordination happens automatically. Therefore, during the initial days, you stop to inhale every time you become aware that you've run out of breath; slowly, with time, you learn to inhale instinctively and more quickly.

Song with breaks

Select a song that you are well versed with; inhale slowly and deeply; sing as many words as you can for as long as the breath lasts. When you run out of air, stop, take another breath and continue from where you left off. Complete the entire song in this manner. Here, basically, the focus is on the respiration as you make multiple stops to inhale.

Song without breaks

Choose another familiar song. Start with a deep, slow breath; now sing the entire song without actually breaking for deep breaths, but rather inhaling quick top-ups of air during the natural pauses in the song. (Natural pauses are the full stops and commas.) It is prudent to go over the song in your mind and make a mental note of the places where you are going to do your top-up inhalations.

The transition from singing one note in one breath to singing the song with excellent breath support is to be made slowly as in the aforementioned series of steps and should take you anywhere between two to three months. As soon as you have learnt the art of singing from the abdomen, it becomes a rather easy task and you can do it intuitively without having to think about it. If you have to keep thinking about the breath as you perform, you are not quite there yet. So, continue practising the above series of steps until the technique becomes second nature to you. This is what I call *drop the technique*. This means let it become a part of your subconscious mode.

Head voice and single notes

After having mastered singing from the abdomen with chest resonance in the last five steps, the same needs to be done for the head voice.

Go to the end of your upper range in the chest voice and take the next note as your head voice. To start with, instead of saying 'Sa', sing it as 'Whooo'. Naturally, do it with your breath coordination. Therefore, the first note of your head voice is after the last note of your chest voice. Scale up the subsequent notes as far as you can go. With enough practice, you should be able to reach at least eight notes, i.e., one octave. Depending upon your natural capabilities, you could perhaps get more notes. The 'whooo' is used because when you utter this particular sound, your vocal cords align themselves into the correct position that is needed for the head voice, i.e., the lower half stationary and the upper half vibrating. Once you have done this well, shift to singing one note in one breath but say them as Sa Re Ga Ma ...

Head voice in jumbled and multiple notes

Do the same exercises indicated for multiple and jumbled notes in the chest voice section. Only, replace chest voice with head voice.

Song with breaks in head voice

Repeat the exercises described in the chest voice section for songs with breaks. Only, replace chest voice with head voice.

Song without breaks in head voice

Repeat the exercises prescribed in the chest voice section for songs without breaks. Only, replace chest voice with head voice.

Using the entire range of your head and chest voices

Here you need to learn to glide easily between the chest voice and the head voice and then back to the chest voice.

So, coordinating with your breath, sing the notes from the lowest note of your chest voice and as you come to a few notes before the end of your range, sing them as 'Aha' ... 'Whoa' and 'Whoo' and then continue as Sa Re Ga Ma into your head voice. This allows an easy transition between the two registers. Once you are well versed with this practice, you can continue to take them as your normal notes and practise the same in songs.

Notes with loudness variation

- Sing alternate notes loud and soft across your entire range keeping the breath in coordination.
- Sing four notes loud and four notes soft, keeping your breath in coordination, across your entire range.
- As you sing the gradient of the notes, gradually increase your volume from the softest to the loudest as a transition, keeping the breath in coordination.

Song with loudness variation

Maintaining breath coordination, sing a song by alternating between loud and soft for each line. This exercise is designed to increase the flexibility and your control over your voice. You do not sing songs like this in your performance; this is just an exercise in flexibility practice.

Song with pitch variation

Pick a familiar song and sing it in your natural pitch with breath coordination. Next sing it in a pitch one octave below your natural pitch; and then, repeat in one octave above your natural pitch. This way, you will know whether you are able to extend your range to almost three octaves.

Notes with resonance variation

Sing all the notes in your range with breath coordination – first, with throat resonance, then, mouth resonance and lastly, nasal resonance.

Song with resonance variation

Sing a song with breath coordination in all three resonances.

6

THE LAWYER'S, CORPORATE EXECUTIVE'S AND CEO'S VOICE

Communication between human beings is important for two reasons: one to share our thoughts and the other to form a relationship. Nowhere is this more relevant than in the corporate world. What we say is very important; but how we say it is perhaps even more so. Both in the corporate world and the world of law, concepts or ideas are of great significance. Equally important is the tone of the voice, the pace and intensity of the talk, the emphasis on certain words and the non-verbal communication that takes place. Almost all of us are sure of what to say, but a successful person is one who is also sure of how to say it.

The main challenge of a CEO, corporate executive or lawyer is to be able to effectively communicate his ideas to his team. The word 'effective' here is key because what he has in mind has to be conveyed and executed. For people in top-level management, apart from voicing skills, language skills with excellent vocabulary and articulation will ensure accurate and succinct expression, especially when they have dialogues with people from other cultures across the globe. The ability to communicate one's thought non-judgementally, without colouring them with biases and prejudices, is imperative.

Time and again, two people doing the same presentation or arguing the same case in court seem to have entirely different outcomes, and one wonders why. Here is where factors like a deep voice, effective use of words, tone of one's voice, judicious emphasis and intonation of key words become significant. Therefore, although content is critical, presentation skills are the mainstay to a successful result. Upcoming lawyers and CEOs are trained to make impressive PowerPoint presentations, how to dress well and carry themselves with self-confidence. Although these are important, for this set of professional voice users, developing a combination of verbal and non-verbal communication skills is de rigueur. Some of these skills are explained below:

DEVELOP A DEEP VOICE

Research has shown that voices of low frequency or baritones seem to grab people's attention more effectively than high-pitched voices. It would be prudent for these voice users to develop a deep, resonant voice. Although content is ultimately the bottom line, a deep, resonant voice sounds authoritative, convincing and captivating.

SLOW DOWN

It is all about pacing oneself and getting the appropriate speed. If you speak too fast, people are going to miss out a lot and if you are too slow, people are going to get bored. It is about finding the right pace and your ability to execute it.

VARY YOUR VOICE

It simply means – don't drone on in a boring monotone so much o that people don't want to listen to what you want to say, even if what you are saying is very important; modulate your voice! Sound interesting, so that people are eager to listen. For a corporate executive, aspects of varying your pitch may not be as important as identifying and emphasizing the key words. So, again, content will guide you to highlight the key words in every slide or paragraph. How to locate these key words and the various methods used to spotlight them in your talk is also explained in detail in the chapter on voice modulation.

Here is a short sample paragraph to demonstrate the best ways to stress on key words to help make your talk interesting and catchy:

'We recommend the setting up of a five-hundred-crore-rupee national fund for the unorganized sector. Two thousand crore rupees are to be pumped into the programme for employment assurance through skill development.'

The key words in this paragraph would be 'five-hundred-crore-rupee', 'employment assurance' and 'skill development'.

REACH OUT TO THE ENTIRE AUDIENCE

Often, it is not just about your voice reaching a very large audience during your elocution. You man have excellent acoustics, amplification systems and microphones that ensure your voice is heard by everybody in the crowd right up to the person in the last row; however, you may find it difficult to capture and hold the people's attention. This reflects directly on the vigour in your voice and the amount of energy you project through your voice to the assembly. If your voice sounds dull, flat, lacklustre or lifeless, the listener tunes out and will not absorb what you are saying. However, if you can infuse vitality into your voice to make it dynamic and animated, and project your voice, you can, irrespective of the content, rest assured that each and every one in the audience is paying attention to you.

DEVELOP STAMINA TO GO ON FOR AN ENTIRE DAY

Stamina of your voice depends upon your breathing skills and voice exercise regimen with a warm-up routine on a daily basis.

Time and again, a corporate executive, a lawyer or a CEO may have to talk, argue or negotiate for hours on end and, after all the effort, the matter may or may not be settled. By this time, even if the person is exhausted, his voice needs to sound fresh and forceful. If the voice starts flagging, it can tip the balance of the talks from success to failure. Only by developing vocal stamina, which is done by improving endurance, can the voice continue to sound compelling and dynamic even after many hours.

BE CLEAR AND DON'T MUMBLE

What you say should come across very clearly. Therefore, good diction and articulation with excellent pronunciation skills are of utmost importance. One may not be aware that one's speech is indistinct; therefore, honest feedback from a colleague or friend should be the order of the day. And then you need to act on that feedback.

ADJUST YOUR VOLUME AND TONE

This is probably the most important aspect of communication skills. More often than not, in our personal and professional interactions, what we say and what we intend to say get, misinterpreted and misunderstood only due to the tone of our voice. If you speak loudly, you could be misunderstood as being overbearing or pushy. If you are too soft, you may be considered a meek pushover. Although what you say is of the essence, how you say it is just as important. Depending on the impression you want to create, pay close attention to your volume and tone. In order to achieve complete control and flexibility of the volume of your voice, work on the basic skill exercises for voice parameters, as mentioned earlier. Let us explore some behavioural emotions and their voice counterparts below.

As a lawyer, corporate executive or CEO, here are some emotions that you can reflect in your voice depending on the situation and your need, and use it to your advantage. Some of them are positive emotions, while others are considered negative. Nonetheless, in the corporate or legal world, both these sets of emotions are often required to be able to communicate effectively.

The positive emotions that one can display and which can be easily grasped by the listener along with their vocal counterparts are:

- Confidence: low-pitched, loud voice with a slow and steady pace
- Optimism: proper diction with medium volume
- Freshness, eagerness or enthusiasm: loud, high-pitched voice with a fast pace
- Warmth and pride: slow pace and loud voice
- Gratitude and honesty: slow pace, low volume with a lot of pauses
- Sympathy and empathy: low volume, low pitch and slow pace and a lot of key words
- Stability, balance and calmness: plenty of key words, with a strong, loud voice

Likewise, the way you use your voice can relay negative emotions even when you don't want to portray them. These are:

- Anger: too loud a voice
- Irritation: extremely fast speech
- Frustration: too many pauses and slow pace

- Fear: low volume, low speed and mumbling
- Arrogance: loud voice, too many stressed words
- Boredom, apathy, detachment: low volume, low speed and no stressed words.

LOOK AT PEOPLE

When you speak to people, apart from all the above-mentioned voicing skills, proper eye contact is a must. Otherwise, it can be misconstrued as diffidence or uncertainty.

WRAP UP

At the end, you need to summarize and wrap up your talk or arguments, so that your message is clearly understood, even if people have been distracted and not heard everything you said.

Here are some more non-verbal communication aspects that need to be kept in mind. These have nothing to do with your voicing skills, but are equally important in the life of a CEO or a lawyer:

- Being assertive
- Being empathetic
- Being prepared to negotiate
- Information gathering
- Listening skills
- Treating a conversation as a two-way street

- Being friendly and polite
- Small talk
- Response versus reaction
- Prodding
- Creating emotional connects
- Encouragement
- Humour
- Orientation towards resolution

7

THE COMPLETE VOCAL EXERCISE GUIDE

LEARN TO BREATHE DEEP

Here is a step-by-step exercise to develop deep breathing:

- Get yourself into a quiet space. Switch off your phone.
- Lie down on your back with your head supported by a pillow and your spine as evenly aligned with the head as possible. Alternatively, you may sit cross-legged and erect. Ensure that you are wearing loose-fitting clothes that will allow your abdomen to move.
- Place one hand on your abdomen and the other on your chest.
- Slowly inhale, take in as much air as you can until you can take in no more. You will notice that your chest and belly inflate, pushing your hands outward.
- Now slowly exhale; let your chest and belly deflate and move inward.

- Ensure that your shoulders are relaxed and still.
- If you are sitting upright, there should be no upward and downward movement of the belly and chest, but rather a forward and inward movement. However, if you are supine, the movement should only be up and down as you respire.
- When you have completed one breath, inhale again for your second breath.
- Repeat for twelve counts before you take a break.
- Repeat the set of twelve deep breaths two more times.
- With time, you will be able to breathe deeply with more ease and also take in more air per breath.
- Once it becomes a habit, you will spontaneously and always breathe deeply.

LEARN TO SPEAK FROM YOUR ABDOMEN

First Week

- Start by doing your deep breathing exercise.
- Sit cross-legged and wear loose-fitting clothes.
- Put one hand on your chest and the other on your lower abdomen.
- Take a deep breath. As you do that, your stomach should distend.
- The shoulders and chest remain still, the breathing, soundless and very relaxed.
- As you exhale, your stomach should deflate fully and tauten.
- This is one deep breath.

- Don't stop. Take the next breath without a break.
- Do this exercise twelve times continuously.
- Take a break and do two more sets.
- Do this twice or thrice a day.
- Also become aware of your breathing throughout the day and consciously make it deeper.

Second Week

- Once you have learnt the above exercise to make your breathing deeper, let's try and harness it for speech.
- Inhale deeply; as you breathe out say 'aa' for as long as the breath lasts.
- Repeat with the sounds 'ee' and 'oo'.
- Now take a deep breath and start counting from one onwards. Say as many numbers as you can in a single breath.
- Continue until you reach a hundred.
- The best way to ascertain whether you are using your breath and speaking from the stomach (not your throat) is if your voice can be increased comfortably – that is, if you can be loud without hurting your throat.

Third Week

- Now, use the same number technique for reading.
- Inhale deeply and read aloud as many words as you can from a book or a newspaper for as long as the breath lasts.
- Stop; then take another breath and continue.

- Continue this exercise until you finish reading four to five pages (approximately 2,000 words).

Fourth Week

- Continue reading, but without stopping for breath except at the natural pauses, i.e., the full-stops, commas, colons, semicolons, etc.
- This way you would have learnt to read by speaking from the abdomen and not from the throat.

EXERCISES FOR PARAMETERS OF VOICE

Here are some exercises to work on the parameters of your voice to improve its flexibility and also aid in modulation.

Weeks One and Two

Loudness exercises

- Mastering the extremes: Take a deep breath and count to five, softly; count from six to ten, loudly. Continue alternating loudness and softness for every five numbers, up to fifty, quickly taking breaths whenever needed.
- Alternating loudness: Count from one to fifty by alternating soft and loud for each number. So, you whisper one, yell out two, a hushed three, a strident four, and so on, until you reach fifty, taking quick breaths as required.
- The train: Count to fifty starting with a very soft voice and gradually increase the volume until you reach the

maximum decibel level; then, gradually decrease the volume until you are barely audible. Take quick breaths whenever needed.

Pitch exercises

- Mastering the extremes: Take a deep breath and count from one to five with low pitch; count from six to ten in a high pitch. Continue alternating low pitch and high pitch for every five numbers, up to fifty, quickly taking breaths as required.
- Alternating pitch: Count from one to fifty by alternating low and high pitch for each number. Therefore, one in baritone, a shrill two, a bass three, a squeaky four, and so on, until you get to fifty, taking breaths whenever needed.
- The train: Count from one to fifty starting with a very low pitch and gradually increase the pitch until you reach your highest note; then, gradually decrease the pitch until you reach your deepest bass; inhale quick breaths as required.

Resonance exercises

- Count from one to fifty predominantly using throat resonance, taking breaths whenever needed.
- Count from one to fifty predominantly using mouth or oral resonance, taking breaths whenever needed.
- Count from one to fifty predominantly using nasal resonance, taking breaths whenever required.

Week Three

Read a newspaper or your script or presentation with alternating loudness in each sentence. That is, whisper one sentence and read the next sentence as loud as you can, and so on. Do the same with pitch and resonance. These exercises do not carry any obvious meaning in terms of modulation or punctuation, but they help to improve the flexibility of the voice and your ability to change the parameters of your voice with ease.

EXERCISES FOR VOICE PROJECTION

Week One

- Relaxation exercises (yawn, sigh).
- Take a deep breath and say one vowel loudly per breath.

Remember that you are not shouting or screaming but saying it out in a very strong voice, from your belly and not from your throat. So, basically, you are creating a contrast between your soft conversational voice and a loud, booming, resonant voice. Imagine a wire extending from your mouth to the corner of the room and project your voice along this line.

Week Two

Repeat exercises one and two of week one.

- Inhale deeply and project your voice as you count three numbers per breath.

- Single words: Take a deep breath and use a single breath to project a single word. You could use a dictionary for a list of words.
- After having mastered the word level, move on to short phrases. Inhale deeply and project the entire phrase.

DICTION EXERCISES

Part One

Since diction calls for flexibility of the tongue, lips, palate, etc., start off by performing simple tongue and lip exercises.

Part Two

- Read the phonetic chart. How do you know you are reading it right? This is one section where you will need verbal guidance from either a teacher or online recordings. As soon as you have mastered the correct pronunciation of each sound, move to the next step.
- Make a list of words with each sound in the beginning of a word, middle of a word and end of a word. Can you guess where you can find such a perfect list? Of course, the dictionary of that particular language. So, start reading the dictionary. The dictionary of any language is the best collection of words with all possible sounds and all possible sound combinations.
- When you have mastered the pronunciation of all sounds at word level, move on to sentence level. Read aloud from any reading material like a book or a

newspaper, keeping in mind the proper pronunciation of all words.

- Make a list of combination sounds. For example, 'st', 'tr', 'ksh', etc. Practise them at the sound level and word levels before moving on to the sentence level. The dictionary is the best place to find all the available combinations in that language.
- The moment you feel that you have done enough practice, it might be a good idea to record your reading and listen to yourself. Ask your teacher, if you have one, or a trusted friend, to check on your pronunciation.
- As soon as you feel you have developed a fairly good diction in the language, you can practise tongue-twisters which will test your pronunciation skills. Here is a small list of tongue twisters in Hindi and in English. Two lists of tongue-twisters, one each in English and Hindi, have been presented in chapter seven, titled 'Diction', which may be referred to for this purpose.

Tongue Twisters

- Six, sick hicks nick six, slick bricks with picks and sticks.
- Picky people pick Peter Pan Peanut Butter; 'tis the peanut butter picky people pick.
- There those thousand thinkers were thinking, 'How did the other three thieves go through?'
- How much pot could a pot-roast roast, if a pot-roast could roast pot?
- Mr Tongue Twister tried to train his tongue to twist and turn and twit and twat to learn the letter 'T'.

- She saw Sheriff's shoes on the sofa. But how sure was she that she saw Sheriff's shoes on the sofa?
- The Smothers brothers' father's mother's brothers are the Smothers brothers' mother's father's other brothers.
- I slit the sheet, the sheet I slit, and on the slit sheet I sit.
- Six, slippery snails slid slowly seaward.
- Gertie's great-grandma grew aghast at Gertie's grammar.
- Imagine an imaginary menagerie manager managing an imaginary menagerie.
- The thirty-three thieves thought that they thrilled the throne throughout Thursday.
- Silly Simon's sitting in a shoe-shine shop. When he sits, he shines, and when he shines, he sits.
- A good cook could cook as much cookies as a good cook who could cook cookies.
- Did Dick Pickens prick his pinkie pickling cheap cling peaches in an inch of pinch or framing his famed French finch photos?
- Who washed Washington's white woollen underwear when Washington's washerwoman went West?

Hindi tongue-twisters

- Madan mohan, malveya madras mein machhli maarte maarte mare
- Chaar Kachari Kachche Chacha,
  Chaar Kachari Pakke.
  Pakki Kachari Kachche Chacha,
  Kachchi Kachari Pakke!

- Raja Gope Gopal Gopaggam Daas
- Khadak Singh ke khadakane se khadakati hain khidkiyan, khidkiyon ke khadakane se khadakata hai Khadak Singh.
- Chandu ke chacha ne chandu ki chachi ko chandni-chowk mein chaandi ki chammach se chatni chackaee.
- Samajh samajh ke samajh ko samjho.
  Samajh samajh ke samajh ko samajhna hi samajh hai.
  Jo samajh ko samajh kar bhi na samajhe
  Voh....kya hai? Nasamajh hai.
- Kaccha papad, pakka papad.
- Mar ham bi gaye, marham ke liye, marham na mila. Hum dum se gaye, humdum ke liye, humdum na mila

COORDINATE BREATHING AND SINGING

One-note, one-breath singing

Take a slow, deep breath and as you exhale, sing the first note 'Sa' at your pitch. Keep the singing loud so that by default you expel air. There are two ways to become aware whether you are using your breath or not. Firstly, the voice will sound stronger and louder when you use your breath. Secondly, you will feel no pressure in the larynx. Gradually, you develop the ability to sense your exhalation and learn to coordinate it with your singing. Repeat this with all the notes in one octave and back – that is Sa going up the scale to the eighth Sa and back. As soon as you are comfortable with this, reach out to the notes in the next octave above and the one below as follows:

Pa Dha Ni ... (Sa Re Ga Ma Pa Dha Ni Sa) ... Re Ga Ma

The notes within the parentheses represent your main octave. You have half an octave on either side, making your range two octaves.

This exercise will also help you determine your range. In due course, with practice, you will be able to further extend by one or two notes at either ends of your range. This exercise is done by taking a fresh breath for every single note.

Multiple notes

Take a long, deep breath and sing four notes as you exhale. Start at the lowest note of your range and continue to the pinnacle. With practice the number of notes you can sing per breath will increase until you can cover the entire octave in a single breath.

Jumbled notes

Take a long, deep breath and practise singing various jumbled notes as you exhale. Here are a few examples:

- Sa Re Ga ... Re Ga Ma ... Ga Ma Pa ... Ma Pa Dha ... Pa Dha Ni ... Dha Ni Sa.
- Sa Re ... Sa Ga ... Sa Ma ... Sa Pa ... Sa Dha ... Sa Ni ... Sa Sa

Repeat these in your entire vocal range. The idea of doing jumbled and multiple notes is to slowly shift your focus from breathing to singing, simultaneously ensuring that breath coordination happens automatically. Therefore, during the initial days, you stop to inhale every time you become aware that you've run out of breath; slowly, with time, you learn to inhale instinctively and more quickly.

Song with breaks

Select a song that you are well versed in, inhale slowly and deeply and sing as many words as you can for as long as the breath lasts. When you run out of air, stop, take another breath and continue from where you left off. Complete the entire song in this manner. Here, basically, the focus is on the respiration as you make multiple stops to inhale.

Song without breaks

Choose another familiar song. Start with a deep, slow breath; now sing the entire song without actually breaking for deep breaths, but rather inhaling quick top-ups of air during the natural pauses in the song. (Natural pauses are the full stops and commas.) It is prudent to go over the song in your mind and make a mental note of the places where you are going to do your top-up inhalations.

The transition from singing one note in one breath to singing the song with excellent breath support is to be made slowly as in the aforementioned series of steps and should take you anywhere between two to three months. As soon as you have learnt the art of singing from the abdomen, it becomes a rather easy task and you can do it intuitively without having to think about it. If you have to keep thinking about your breath as you perform, you are not quite there yet. So, continue practising the above series of steps until the technique becomes second nature to you. This is what I call *drop the technique*. This means: let it become a part of your subconscious mode.

Head voice and single notes

After having mastered singing from the abdomen with chest resonance in the last five steps, the same needs to be done for the head voice.

Go to the end of your upper range in the chest voice and take the next note as your head voice. To start with, instead of saying 'Sa', sing it as 'Whoo'. Naturally, do it with breath coordination. Therefore, the first note of your head voice is after the last note of your chest voice. Scale up the subsequent notes as far as you can go. With enough practice, you should be able to reach at least eight notes, i.e., one octave. Depending on your natural capabilities, you could perhaps get more notes. The 'whoo' is used because when you say this particular word, your vocal cords align themselves into the correct position that is needed for the head voice, i.e., the lower half stationary and the upper half vibrating. Once you have done this well, shift to singing one note in one breath but say them as Sa Re Ga Ma ...

Head voice in jumbled and multiple notes

Do the same exercises indicated for multiple and jumbled notes in the chest voice section. Only, replace chest voice with head voice.

Song with breaks in head voice

Repeat the exercises described in the chest voice section for songs with breaks. Only, replace chest voice with head voice.

Song without breaks in head voice

Repeat the exercises prescribed in the chest voice section for songs without breaks. Only, replace chest voice with head voice.

Using the entire range of your head and chest voices

Here you need to learn to glide easily between the chest voice and the head voice and then back to the chest voice. So, coordinating with your breath, sing the notes from the lowest note of your chest voice and as you come to a few notes before the end of your range, sing them as 'Aha' ... 'Whoa' and 'Whoo' and then continue as Sa Re Ga Ma into your head voice. This allows an easy transition between the two registers. Once you are well versed with this practice, you can continue to take them as your normal notes and practise the same in songs.

Notes with loudness variation

- Sing alternate notes loud and soft across your entire range, keeping the breath in coordination.
- Sing four notes loud and four notes soft, keeping your breath in coordination, across your entire range.
- As you sing the gradient of the notes, gradually increase

your volume from the softest to the loudest as a transition, keeping the breath in coordination with your singing.

Song with loudness variation

Maintaining breath coordination, sing a song by alternating between loud and soft for each line. This exercise is designed to increase flexibility and control over your voice. You do not sing songs like this in your performance; this is just an exercise in flexibility practice.

Song with pitch variation

Pick a familiar song and sing it in your natural pitch with breath coordination. Next sing it in a pitch one octave below your natural pitch; and then, repeat in one octave above your natural pitch. This way, you will know whether you are able to extend your range to almost three octaves.

Notes with resonance variation

Sing all the notes in your range with breath coordination – first, with throat resonance, then, mouth resonance and lastly, nasal resonance.

Song with resonance variation

Sing a song with breath coordination in all three resonances.

INSTRUCTIONS FOR THE DAY OF PERFORMANCE

Instructions to be followed on the day of a concert/presentation/recording:

- Take voice rest for 3–4 hours prior to the concert. (Complete voice rest – no talking at all).
- Half-an-hour before the performance, do your warm-up exercises.
- Resume minimal talking half an hour prior to the concert.
- Drink plenty of water.
- Eat natural foods (fruits and vegetables).
- Avoid taking any medication.
- Avoid coffee/tea/alcohol.
- Avoid strenuous physical exercises.
- Get plenty of rest and sleep on the previous day.
- A mixture of honey and warm water may be consumed at regular intervals during the concert.
- Immediately after the concert, do your cool-down exercises, and then take complete voice rest for two hours.

WARM-UPS FOR PERFORMANCE OR REHEARSAL

You may be familiar with the concept of doing vocal warm-ups prior to rehearsing or performing. But perhaps you haven't been given enough input about the reasons for this, what and how to do them, and for how long. With the information below, you will gain a better understanding of the importance and benefits of vocal warm-ups (and cool-downs) as well as simple and effective exercises.

Think of Yourself as An Athlete

The guiding principle for all athletes prior to putting strenuous demands on their muscles is that they must be warmed up and limbered. Since your instrument is a part of your body, you can consider yourself a vocal athlete. From this viewpoint, it is perfectly logical to do warm-up exercises to tone the muscles of your instrument before the rigorous demands of the vocal performance.

The production of your voice relies on your breath and the minutely coordinated movements of many muscles. The external muscles of your ribcage and throat as well as the internal muscles of your larynx, tongue, inner throat, and soft palate, to name but a few, must be in good shape and tough enough to weather the excesses of the performance.

Everyone is different, therefore each person's workouts need to be tailored individually. Furthermore, one's warm-up routines may need to vary on a day-to-day basis according to the nature of the performance or rehearsal. The time of day and the condition of your body and voice also influence your warm-up. Some singers develop an exact, never-varying routine that fits their needs no matter what. However, the more tools you have, the better you will be able to modify the perfect warm-up routine each time to suit your needs.

After a proper vocal warm-up, you will be able to start your rehearsal or performance in high gear, rather than the all too usual feeble first two or three songs or pages of the script. The idea is to stretch, tone and limber your vocal muscles so that they are ready to respond to your smallest commands. This is true whether you are a singer or an actor. Treat your voice with respect. Try to stay objective and patient. Warm-ups help you save (not wreck) your voice; they promote performance excellence and career longevity.

Your Six-step Warm-up Routine

Breathing

Your body's breathing mechanism plays a major role in singing. The following exercise is the first in a series designed to stretch and tone the muscles that are vital to this important function. Throughout this exercise keep your mouth open and throat relaxed so that your breathing is unrestricted and occurs naturally in response to the stretch and release of your ribs.

- Stand relaxed but erect, with your arms hanging by your sides.
- Face the wall directly in front of your body; turn your palms forward.
- Open your mouth slightly and keep it open through the entire exercise.
- Stretch your arms up and out to the sides of your body as you slowly raise them. (As you stretch your arms outwards and upwards, inhale through your mouth.)
- Continue stretching and raising your arms upwards from your shoulders; angle them slightly forward and let your palms meet, as though you were going to dive into a pool of water. Your outstretched arms will lift your shoulders and elongate your back muscles. (Your

face should be forward, not raised. If your stomach is tense, let it relax.)

- Silently count from one to six while continuing to stretch up. (Keep your mouth open and throat relaxed. Do not breathe in or out.)
- Now let your arms down faster than you raised them, bringing them down the same way you brought them up. Exhale naturally through your open mouth as you lower your arms.

Repeat these seven steps for a total of twenty times. Take a few minutes' rest after the tenth time, about fifteen minutes. For best results, the exercise should be done on a daily basis.

Face and Neck Massage

Your sounds is produced within the throat by the varied vibrations of the vocal folds. Relaxed muscles of the neck permit the inner vocal muscles to move with greater ease.

- Reflect on some pleasant thought or memory or just take on a peaceful state of mind. As you do each step, breathe slowly and deeply.
- Begin by massaging the muscles of your face. With the fingers of both hands, start at the top and centre of your forehead. In a circular motion, massage the sides of your forehead, down to your ears. Massage your jaw in front of your ears, and then your cheeks, under your eyes and chin. Concentrate your massage on these areas until you feel the muscles soften and relax.

- Next, massage the muscles of your neck. Use the fingers of both hands. Start just under the back of your head. On either side of your spine, stroke down to your shoulders in one smooth or several short motions. Continue until relaxed.
- From the back of your neck, use a few fingers of each hand and begin stroking forward to the sides of your neck. Repeat this motion as many times as necessary until you feel the muscles relax.
- Beginning just behind your jaw on both sides of your neck, stroke downwards towards your shoulders. Repeat as many times as you wish. Work slowly and carefully. Continue until any soreness is gone.
- With the fingers of both hands, use a short forward stroke on the muscles directly below and under the corners of your jaw. As you feel them relax, work forward to under your chin. Repeat this from the corners of your jaw. Do not push or poke. Maintain a slow, gentle touch and don't forget to breathe!

Tongue Relaxer

Singing and speaking with relaxed muscles at the back of the tongue plays an important part in your voice sounding resonant and free. These next exercises will help you improve the tone and projection of your voice.

Open your mouth slightly. Slowly stretch your tongue down and out while letting it remain relaxed. When extended as far forward as possible, slowly stretch it over to one side. Return it to its stretched and forward position.

Slowly stretch it to the other side. Return to the central stretched position. Now slowly retract it into your mouth. Swallow. Do this sequence only once or twice. It can be repeated later in the day, but don't overdo it. The tongue consists of muscles that can get strained!

Lip Trills

Although this may at first feel silly to do, lip trills provide a wonderful massage for your entire vocal tract (specifically the lips, cheeks, tongue, soft palate, back wall of your throat and larynx). We will be using vibration to massage your inner instrument. If you have a tendency to tense your throat muscles when singing or speaking, this can help.

- Take a breath.
- With your lips lightly together, slowly and gently exhale just enough so that your lips begin flapping like a motorboat.
- Do this for as long as you can.
- Take a breath and repeat. Work on lengthening the amount of time you can do this in one breath. When you have repeated this several times successfully, your lip and cheek muscles should feel energized and relaxed.

Sustained Hums

- Take a deep breath.
- Gently hum a pitch in your mid-range. Do this for as long as you can.

- Time yourself with the second hand of a clock. See how many seconds you can sustain the hum. Repeat several times.

Resonance Wake-up

This warm-up does as its name suggests! It wakes up the resonance of your voice. It is also excellent for examining and developing the use of each of the basic vowel sounds used in singing. This exercise uses a series of different vowel and consonant combinations. As you do this, use a basic speaking volume only, on a comfortable mid-range pitch. The consonant will be 'NG'. You shape this consonant with the back of your tongue and soft palate. The back of your tongue raises and lightly meets your soft palate. To find this, say the word 'sing' and sustain the 'NG' position at the end of the word.

- Take a breath. With your mouth kept slightly open and unmoving, keep the tip of your tongue resting against the back of your bottom teeth.
- Put the back of your tongue in the 'NG' position and begin sustaining a comfortable mid-range pitch.
- Feel the vibration shimmer along the roof of your mouth.
- Sustaining the same pitch, change to an 'AH' vowel (pronounced as in 'wand'). The back of your tongue will naturally lower and relax as you sustain the 'AH' vowel.
- On the same breath, alternate the 'NG' consonant with the vowel as many times as you can, NG-AH, NG-AH,

NG-AH, etc.

- Repeat using the same vowel until you experience muscle relaxation in the back of your mouth and throat. Then go to the next NG-vowel combination. The sequence goes as follows:

  - NG-AH (Wand)
  - NG-EE (Seem)
  - NG-A (Same)
  - NG-AA (Apple)
  - NG-EH (When)
  - NG-UH (Some)
  - NG-I (Him)

  During the next two, be sure you do not shape your lips for the sound. It can be achieved by thinking the vowel sound and letting it naturally resonate against the back wall of your mouth/throat.

  - NG-OH (Home)
  - NG-OO (Soon)

COOLING DOWN YOUR VOICE

To use the analogy of the athlete again, a demanding use of muscles fills them with blood and waste products. This is true of the muscles of your vocal folds as well. You can reduce the chance of vocal fatigue and huskiness by using a cool-down to return your vocal folds to their everyday speaking condition.

Cool-down Suggestions

Out of the above exercises, lip trills and short sustained hums are recommended. Also try gently sliding your voice up and down a melodic interval of a third or fifth using the vowel sounds 'ee' and 'ah'. This means doing the hums in your entire octave or jumping the notes like Hum Sa, then Hum Dha, then Sa, then Ni and so on. Cool-downs must be done at a very low (but not whispering) volume so that your vocal folds are gently vibrating. Cool down until your voice feels and sounds normal.

Vocal warm-up should be done close to the time of performing. Vocal exercises should be done some hours earlier, followed by a vocal rest on the days you are rehearsing or performing. Vocal exercises develop your voice while warm-ups prepare it for performance. A warm-up routine lasts anywhere between ten to thirty minutes. Cool-down is usually five to ten minutes.

DAILY EXERCISES FOR VOCAL FITNESS

Breathing Exercises (half an hour every day)

Abdominal breathing

Sit cross-legged on the floor. Close your eyes and focus on your breathing. Inhale through the nose. As you inhale, place a hand on your abdomen – it should come forward. Now, exhale through your mouth, and your abdomen should be sucked in.

Breathing through one nostril

With your thumb, close one nostril. Inhale through the other. At the end of respiration, close the other nostril also. Now, hold your breath as long as you can, keeping both nostrils closed. Exhale through the other nostril. Continue similarly, alternating between both the nostrils.

Humming

Inhale through your nose. As you exhale, hum until the end of the respiration.

Tongue Exercises (five minutes every day): Relaxing the tongue

Here are three short exercises to help limber and tone some of the important muscles that control your vocal apparatus. Just ensure that you accomplish each of the positions and movements of these exercises slowly, relaxing the related muscles as you proceed.

The tongue is a strong muscle for its size but it can get strained. It doesn't need strengthening. It does need gentle limbering so that it can be naturally relaxed as you sing. Each of the following exercises must be done slowly. When stretching, use the tip rather than pulling from the back of your tongue. Your objective is to limber and gradually stretch rather than tense or strain. At the end of each exercise, swallow. This permits the root of your tongue to return to its normal relaxed position.

Serpent tongue

There are seven steps to this exercise. Hold each position for about two seconds. Open your mouth slightly. Keep your lips relaxed. Slowly stretch your tongue out and down while concentrating on letting the back of it remain relaxed. While extended as far forward as possible without strain, slowly stretch it to the left. Return it to the centre, stretching it down and out. Slowly stretch it to the right. Return it to the centre, extending it downwards. Now slowly bring it back inside your mouth. Swallow. Repeat two more times. Do not repeat for more than a total of three times in a row.

Tongue roll

Press the tip of your tongue behind your lower teeth. Keep it there as you roll the body of your tongue forward until you feel a slight stretch of the back of your tongue. Return your tongue inside your mouth, relax it and swallow. Repeat this stretch two more times only. More may create muscle strain.

Resonance wake-up

Open your mouth slightly. Extend your tongue and let it lie on top of your lower lip. With your tongue stretching forward in this position, sustain an 'Ah' tone. Ensure you use an 'Ah' as in the pronunciation of 'want'. Now bring your tongue back to a normal position, pick a higher note and sustain a sung 'Ah'. Repeat this alternately, several times. You should experience a sense of more space in the back of your throat with added muscle relaxation and resonance.

Now try singing. It should feel easier and sound full of resonance. These three tongue exercises are part of a series of warm-ups and vocal-muscle agility exercises which I have developed over the years. You can do these exercises several times during the day, especially before singing.

Neck Exercises

Move your neck very slowly as follows:

- Up and down
- Side to side
- Rotate clockwise
- Rotate anti-clockwise

AFTERWORD

We have now come to the end of the book and I sincerely hope that I have managed to achieve what I set out to do. As mentioned earlier, my aim in writing this book was to introduce both the common man and the professional voice user to his voice – from understanding how the voice is produced, to its various attributes and voice associations like diction, accents and modulation, to what could go wrong with your voice and on to voice building. Whether you are an actor, singer, news presenter, corporate executive, lawyer or teacher, this book holds valuable information and knowledge for you. My purpose of writing this book would have been achieved irrespective of whether you glance through this book casually, go only to the sections that are pertinent to you, or use it like a textbook to enhance your voice skills.

My emphasis in the book has been to tell professional voice users not to take their voice for granted, but to protect it as much as possible. The voice is a very delicate asset and one that is prone to trouble you or let you down at crunch time. Apart from producing embarrassment at not being able to perform when required, not taking care and not enhancing your skills could also lead to vocal damage and prolonged and frustrating therapeutic treatments. Nowhere is the adage 'an ounce of prevention is worth a pound of cure' more relevant than in the world of voice users.

My final ten commandments to professional voice users would be to:

- Take your voice seriously.
- Understand the how and why of voice.
- Do your voice exercises daily.
- Strictly follow the dos and don'ts for voice usage.
- Always do your vocal warm-ups and cool-downs.
- Remember that the backbone of your voice is good, deep breathing.
- Never ever shout or scream no matter how upset you are.
- Love your voice, give it your kind attention and see how it loves you back.
- Seek a good voice teacher and keep using his or her professional services all your life.
- Read this book over and over again, until every chapter becomes an intrinsic part of you and you become your voice.

ACKNOWLEDGEMENTS

I wish to thank my husband, Dr Vaidyanathan, for his constant love and support, not only for the book but for everything. I also thank my son, Arvind, for being an inspiration in helping me excel.

I express my sincere gratitude to the following people for giving me an opportunity to work in my chosen field consistently and thus grow in knowledge and strength – Shankar Mahadevan, Sridhan Ranganathan, Shernaz Patel, Subhash Ghai, Kishore Namit Kapoor, Dr Sanjeev Badhwar, Dr Nupur Nerurkar Kapoor and Ameen Sayani.

I wish to thank Dr James P. Thomas in Portland, USA, for mentoring me and sharing his knowledge and wisdom. His generosity in opening up his world of voice to me was unmatched.

I wish to thank all my teachers from Mumbai's B.Y.L. Nair Hospital for not only educating me in the field of speech pathology, but also for instilling in me sincerity, perseverance, determination and direction.

ACKNOWLEDGEMENTS

I would like to express my thanks to Shoabha Pattabhiraman for doing a wonderful job on the illustrations in the book. I am grateful to my parents and my sisters for their unconditional love and believing in my capabilities and talents.

I am thankful to my mother-in-law, Mrs Muthulakshmi, for being my first music teacher and teaching me everything I know about music today.

I express my gratitude to my friend and spiritual guide Manoj Khatri for his presence in my life.

I wish to thank my friends – Aparna, for her constant love and support, and Narayan, for opening my mind to infinite possibilities.

I am grateful to my friends and family – Samir Sikri, Alan Mans, Nishita, Meenakshi, Jagruti, Kumar, Sarita, Suresh and Sunita, for their love and support.

Thanks also to my agent, Priya Doraswamy, for her constant guidance without which this book would not have been possible. At HarperCollins India, I'm glad I have Debasri Rakshit as my editor and I'm thankful to her team for all the support in publishing this book and taking it places.

The
AYURVEDIC
Diet
REENITA MALHOTRA HORA

FEEL FIT
LOOK FANTASTIC
IN 3·2·1
by Hollywood celebrity trainer
Ramona
BRAGANZA
GET MOTIVATED!
Learn to eat and train like the stars!

START UP Your Restaurant

THE DEFINITIVE GUIDE FOR ANYONE WHO DREAMS OF RUNNING THEIR OWN RESTAURANT

JAYANTH NARAYANAN
PRIYA BALA